I0881077

GERMAN BREAKTHROUGH IN GREECE

THE 1941 BATTLE OF THE PINEIOS GORGE

THEN AND NOW

GERMAN BREAKTHROUGH IN GREECE

THE 1941 BATTLE OF THE PINEIOS GORGE

THEN AND NOW

By Jeffrey Plowman

AFTER THE BATTLE

An Imprint of Pen & Sword Books Ltd

German Breakthrough in Greece. The 1941 Battle of the Pineios Gorge – Then and Now
Copyright © After the Battle and Jeffrey Plowman, 2024

Published by After the Battle
An imprint of Pen & Sword Books Ltd
47 Church Street, Barnsley,
South Yorkshire, S70 2AS
Tel. 01226 734222
Fax. 01226 734438
Email: enquiries@pen-and-sword.co.uk
Website: **www.afterthebattle.com**
www.pen-and-sword.co.uk

Printed and bound in India by Parksons Graphics Pvt. Ltd.

ISBN: 9781399079051

Commissioning Editor: Rob Green
Editor: Karel Margry
Design: Paul Wilkinson
Cover design: Jon Wilkinson

The right of Jeffrey Plowman to be identified as the author of this Work has been asserted by him in accordance with the Copyright, Designs and Patents Act 1988.

Credits:
This book is a greatly expanded version of two articles by the same author previously published in *After the Battle* magazine, issue 194 (February 2022): 'Breakthrough at the Pinios Gorge' and 'The Sinking of the *Kybfels* and *Marburg*'.

Acknowledgements:
I wish to thank the following people for their help in the preparation of this manuscript: Pier Paolo Battistelli for making available German Army photographs he obtained from Record Group 242 (Foreign Records Seized) at the US National Archives; Terry Brown, Aaron Fox, Peter Cooke, Perry Rowe and Malcolm Thomas for accessing files from Archives New Zealand; Peter Brown, Rob Green and Winston Ramsey for accessing files from The National Archives in the UK; Martin Block for the war diaries and combat reports of the 2. Panzer-Division; George Handrinos for photographs and material on Greek railways; Karel Margry for sourcing photographs from the German Bundesarchiv and editorial assistance; Phil Deed for access to Harry Capamagain's diary; Jason Lowe for details from Francis Clive Lowe's diary; Stephen Hutcheon for the account of his uncle Jack Greaves and photographs, and Sarah Ball for cleaning up some of the images. I also wish to thank Stefano di Giusto, Ioannis Delfos, John Irwin, Lee Archer, Mark McKenzie, Chris Papageorgiou, Mike Smythe, Nikos Stavropoulos, Franz Steinzer, Akira Takiguchi and Antonis Voutsinos for photographs, and Nikos Valasiadis for taking additional comparison photos.

I am also grateful to the following organisations for assistance with information and photographs: the Alexander Turnbull Library, Archives New Zealand, the Australian War Memorial, the Bundesarchiv, the National Archives in the UK and the National Archives and Records Administration in the US. I am also thankful for all the help I have received from members of the *WWII History in Greece* Facebook page.

I am especially grateful to my wife, Yvonne, who willingly accompanied me to Greece in the knowledge that I wanted to visit the two battlefields that feature prominently in this book.

Photo Credit Abbreviations:
ATL – Alexander Turnbull Library; AWM – Australian War Memorial; BA – Bundesarchiv; NIOD – Nederlands Instituut voor Oorlogsdocumentatie; USNA – US National Archives. Unless specified otherwise, all illustrations are from the *After the Battle* archive.

Front Cover: A Panzer III of the 2. Kompanie of Panzer-Regiment 3 of the 2. Panzer-Division fording the Pineios river in the Pineios gorge on April 18, 1941 – then and now. (USNA/John Irwin)

Back Cover:
Top: A Panzer III of the 1. Kompanie of Panzer-Regiment 3 abandoned on the saddle track past Platamon Castle after it ran onto a mine during the German attack on Platamon ridge on April 17, 1941 – then and now. (Jeffrey Plowman Collection/Nikos Valasiadis)

Centre: An A10 Cruiser tank from No. 9 Troop of C Squadron of the 3rd Royal Tank Regiment, part of the British 1st Armoured Brigade, abandoned north of Kozani due to a broken fuel pump on April 14, 1941 during W Force's retreat to the south – then and now. (Robert Gregory Collection/Google)

Bottom: A German motorcycle combination passing a Guy Quad Ant artillery tractor and 25-pounder gun of the 4th NZ Field Regiment that got stuck in the ford through the Nessonis swamp during the Anzac Corps' retreat to Larissa on the night of April 18/19, 1941 – then and now. (Robert Gregory Collection/Google)

CONTENTS

A PzKpfw II from Regimental Headquarters of Panzer-Regiment 3 of the 2. Panzer-Division in the Pineios Gorge on the morning of April 17, 1941. (USNA StB 144-31)

INTRODUCTION

ONE THING NOTICEABLE from studies of the Second World War is that in any military operation or campaign there seems to be one battle that defines it, whether it be one on the cusp of success or defeat, such as Maleme on Crete in 1941, or for the controversial decisions surrounding its execution, such as Monte Cassino in Italy in 1944. Thus, in the case of the ill-fated expeditionary force Britain sent in 1941 to support the Greeks against Axis aggression, the battle for the Pineios gorge comes to the fore, not just for the intensity of the fighting but for the controversy that came to develop afterwards between Australia and New Zealand.

This came on top of the fact that the entire British involvement in Greece was, in itself, controversial. Just why the British Prime Minister, Winston Churchill, persisted in his efforts to help Greece at that time is not clear. With the British army struggling to recover from catastrophic losses of materiel, in particular those suffered in the battle for France in 1940, it would seem that his desire to take on a new venture in the Balkans was overstretching the resources of Britain and of the Commonwealth nations that supplied troops. That this occurred at a time when his Western Desert Force under Lieutenant-General Richard O'Connor had just achieved considerable success over the Italians in Libya in securing the entire Cyrenaica region defies belief. Whether, of course, O'Connor's men could have gone on to take the rest of Libya is another matter but to have diluted the effort of the Western Desert Force to aid Greece seemed reckless, especially when there were also threats from other places, including Somalia, Syria and Iraq.

Nevertheless, the British eventually did send the Greeks two infantry divisions and an armoured brigade even though they were well aware there was a high chance that at some time in the future these might have to be evacuated. They also did so with full knowledge of the disparities in both quality and numbers in both their armour and air support. Thus, from the time this expeditionary force (known as W Force) set foot in Greece it became apparent that they lacked the resources to hold the defensive line they had agreed on with the Greeks. In fact their first moves, following the invasion of Greece by German troops on April 6, was a controlled retreat to a more-defensible line running along the Olympus mountain range, the passes of which they assigned to brigade-group sized forces. In spite of these moves, there were still two substantial holes in this line, one at Kalabaka in the west and the other at Platamon ridge on the Aegean coast. They eventually plugged the latter with a single infantry battalion with a mere troop of artillery for support.

The full significance of the Platamon-Pineios region appears to have evaded the higher levels of command in W Force, despite its historic imperative. Platamon ridge, along with the Pineios river gorge to its south, is a strategically important location that offers access to the Plains of Thessaly from the Aliákmon river valley of Lower Macedonia. A testament to this was the fact that the Crusaders built a castle on the top of Platamon ridge sometime between 1204 and 1222. The Pineios gorge, also known as the Vale of Tempi or referred to as the Wolf's Throat by the Byzantines, had been the scene of numerous battles in history, one of the earliest being between the Romans and King Perseus of Macedon in 169 BC. In contrast to the high command of W Force, the Germans were quick to recognise this strategically important route and sent an armoured force against the weak defensive group that W Force had deployed there. In doing so they threatened Larissa, a city which was the only avenue of escape for all of the Anzac forces along the Olympus mountain range and even for the ad hoc unit (known as Savige Force) that had been hastily assembled and sent to Kalabaka. Despite all this, the Anzacs managed to escape the trap but only just, leaving behind dumps of food and petrol, though not enough of the latter for the Germans to mobilise an armoured pursuit column.

Just how the Anzacs succeeded in holding the Pineios defile long enough to allow their forces to escape the trap has been the subject of a number of articles and books over the years, yet the root causes of the failure on both the Anzac and Axis side of the equation are still not clear. This has not been helped by the selective use of material from primary sources either. For instance, when the 21st New Zealand Battalion history was written in 1953 the author simply ignored Lieutenant Michael O'Neil's detailed account of No. 13 Platoon at Pineios, the official account simply stating that the platoon 'was overwhelmed in a cloud of dust and smoke' when the panzers reached their position. The matter has also been coloured by some of the acrimony that developed between the Australian and New Zealand historians involved in the preparation the official histories of this campaign. One complaint that came to the fore repeatedly in Australian accounts was the need for an Australian battalion commander to draw his revolver twice to halt the retreat of some New Zealand field artillery, while conveniently ignoring a unit war diary account that the guns were out of ammunition. Disputes like this have continued to the present day. A case in point is the loss of telephone contact with Lieutenant-Colonel Neil Macky of the 21st NZ Battalion. This seems to have been of concern to the Australians, particularly as it occurred around the time that Macky's men were seen climbing away from the fighting on the hills overlooking Tempi. One quote favoured by Australian historians read: 'Tanks are through the village and we are withdrawing to the hills', yet it was only one of three different versions in the Australian war diary. It is also at odds with German combat reports. At least there is consensus between historians of both nations over who was primarily to blame, both settling on Macky and his battalion on what has been described as a shambolic defence of Pineios gorge after an exemplary defence of Platamon ridge and agreeing on how quickly the unit collapsed after the first appearance of the tanks.

This is an interesting point because in order to determine how quickly 21st Battalion's defence disintegrated, particularly in comparison to the two Australian battalions involved, it is necessary to establish a precise timeline of events on April 18, which is something that no narrative to date has successfully achieved. Yet this information was readily available from German sources, certainly at the time the official histories were being prepared.

There is also a general lack of awareness of the nature of the terrain in

Panzer IIIs of the I. Abteilung of Panzer-Regiment 3 of the 2. Panzer-Division using the railway line along the Pineios river to advance through the Pineios gorge on April 17, 1941. (BA Bild 101I-162-0293-27a)

the area of the fighting. Howard Kippenberger, the Editor-in-Chief of the New Zealand official histories, was particularly critical of 21st Battalion's defensive positions, though he never had, apparently, visited the area. For instance, official accounts stating that the platoon defending the demolitions in the gorge could have clambered 200 metres up above the road are not consistent with the topography in the area. An appreciation of this could only have been gained by visiting the area in person or, these days, by reference to the Streetview feature of Google Maps. Matching the wartime photographs with modern-day comparisons – the format of all *After the Battle* publications – is also a further aid to understanding certain parts of the battle, for example how the Germans actually got their tanks over the Pineios river, particularly in a gorge where the steep terrain and constriction of the river flow would have provided few opportunities for this.

One aspect of the campaign in Greece that has not received much attention is the role of Ultra – i.e. intelligence obtained from decrypts of intercepted German army radio and teleprinter messages –, especially since this was the very first time in the war that comprehensive appreciations based on Ultra decrypts were transmitted to commanders in the field. For the Greek campaign there were two sets of Ultra intercepts available, the German Army and Air force series (HW 5/9 and 5/11) and the Admiralty intercepts for German, Italian and Japanese radio communications (DEFE 3/891). When discussing Ultra it is essential to remember that dissemination of its contents was extremely restricted. For security reasons, to safeguard the secret that the enemy's codes had been broken, information from Ultra was only made available to headquarters of Army level and above – in this case GHQ Middle East (General Archibald Wavell) and GHQ W Force (General Henry Maitland Wilson). It never went lower than that, so neither the commander of the Anzac Corps in Greece (Lieutenant-General Thomas Blamey) nor any of the division commanders, let alone brigade or battalion commanders, were privy to it.

The chance to look into German command

decisions and changes in strategy would have helped Wilson redefine his response to them – depending of course on how many of the Ultra decrypts actually reached him as there were communication issues between his advanced headquarters and W Force Headquarters in Athens. Most of the 150 or so signals deciphered during the Greek campaign contained only tactical information, identifying German spearhead units and their locations, which was useful but quickly outdated and left little time to base strategic decisions on. However, a few messages were of grander importance. For instance, from signals in the HW 5/11 series Wilson first learned of the German plans to bypass his main defensive line through the Monastir gap on April 8; this was also the source of his intelligence on April 15 of their intention to operate south of Olympus. The latter signal prompted him to bring forward the withdrawal to the Thermopylae Line by a day – a timely intervention that, in the opinion of the Australians, avoided a disaster for W Force. The Ultra intercepts from the Greek campaign, notably those from the DEFE 3/891 series (which have an OL prefix), provide interesting tactical details from the German side not available elsewhere, hence we have included reference to them at several places in the main narrative (giving the decrypt's OL number and its date and time of origin).

When it all comes down to it, the battle for the Pineios gorge was a small, obscure battle in a relatively unknown part of Greece that formed part of a campaign that should never have really happened. So why tell this story? For me the fascinating thing was that this was the first time that Australian and New Zealand forces had come together in combat in an Anzac force since the First World War and provided an opportunity to examine how they fared against the Germans, particularly in relation to the performance of the British Expeditionary Force in France the previous year. On the surface they did appear to perform well, particularly in defence, something the Germans were willing to acknowledge in their post-action reports. But scratch the surface and this view starts to unravel, particularly in the area of command and control, and what happened at the Pineios gorge is a prime example of that. While the troops on the ground fought well and were instrumental in delaying the Germans long enough to allow the entire Anzac Corps to escape the trap, it is the missteps that kept occurring at the higher level of command that are disturbing. Some have commented that this could be put down to the decision to place into positions of command men whose only experience of war was the previous one and that is an interesting point. Whatever the case, the Anzacs came the closest they ever could to disaster at the Pineios gorge than at any other time in Greece. The story that emerges is a fascinating mixture of German overconfidence, logistical and tactical errors, coupled with Anzac command intransigence and, at times, sheer desperate combat.

THE STAGE IS SET

THE BRITISH INVOLVEMENT in the Balkans can be traced back to the start of the Second World War when Winston Churchill, the British Prime Minister, and Albert Lebrun, the French President, offered to support Greece against the Axis, a stance Churchill maintained even after the fall of France in June 1940. When Italy launched an attack on Epirus from Albania on November 13, 1940, the Greek Prime Minister, General Ioannis Metaxas, was reluctant to accept ground forces from Britain. He did, however, let the British occupy Crete, allowing him to redeploy the Crete Division to the Albanian front. At Churchill's insistence a British Military Mission was also established with the Greek Army, initially under Major-General Michael Gambier-Parry, but it was only given one opportunity to reconnoitre the threatened areas of Thrace and eastern Macedonia before the Greeks vetoed further visits there. In the end the Italian offensive stalled and soon turned into a retreat as the Greek army swept back into Albania.

In January 1941, prompted by this and Enigma intercepts that led the British to suspect an invasion of Greece was imminent, General Archibald Wavell, the Commander-in-Chief of Middle East Command, flew to Athens with Air Chief Marshall Arthur Longmore, his air force commander, to conduct negotiations with Metaxas and his army commander General Alexander Papagos. Despite the fact that Greece's effort to reinforce their forces in Bulgaria had left them only with four weak divisions on the Bulgarian border, they were still reluctant to accept the British offer of ground forces, considering it inadequate. Their thinking was that this might precipitate a German invasion of their country. Instead they were hoping that an alliance with Yugoslavia would help crush the Italians in a pincer movement. The Yugoslavs, however, proved less than willing to become involved. Given this, it was not surprising that the British negotiations with the Greeks were not particularly successful and all they could agree on was the dispatch of some squadrons of light bombers and fighters to Greece.

Following the sudden death of Metaxas on January 29, his successor Alexander Koryzis re-opened negotiations with the British. As a result Wavell was ordered to secure Cyrenaica in Libya with the minimum of forces and assemble another force for deployment in Greece. For the latter he chose the British 1st Armoured Brigade (Brigadier Harold Charrington), the New Zealand Division (Major-General Bernard Freyberg), the 6th Australian Division (Major-General Iven Mackay) and the 7th Australian Division (Lieutenant-General John Lavarack).

Just how this force was actually raised, however, was somewhat convoluted. Wavell made his first approach to the Australian Prime Minister, Robert

In March 1941, the British sent an expeditionary force, dubbed W Force, to Greece. While the Greeks chose to hold onto the Metaxas Line, W Force and other Greek troops took up positions along the Aliákmon Line, further west and at right angle to the Greek border, these dispositions being predicated on the German attack being launched from Bulgaria. In the event, part of the Germans forces launched their offensive by going through Yugoslavia first, thus circumventing the Metaxas Line. (Wikipedia)

Menzies, on February 10, when the latter was on stopover in the Middle East on his way to Great Britain, there to seek reinforcements for Australia. At that stage though, Wavell only talked to Menzies in broad terms of having 'a certain latitude over the deployment of Australian forces'. Menzies then flew to Benghazi where he raised this matter with Lieutenant-General Thomas Blamey, the commander of the Australian Imperial Force, who expressed the view that Australian forces should be treated as under a national command. Menzies then returned to Cairo where he learned, in another meeting with Wavell, of his plans for supporting the Greeks. Unfortunately, though the exact details of that meeting are unknown it would appear that Menzies did not say anything to block Wavell's plans to deploy Australian troops there.

Both Blamey and Freyberg did not find out about Wavell's plans for their troops until February 17, Blamey initially from his liaison officer at General Headquarters in Cairo, news he received with some disquiet. When Freyberg was informed of Wavell's plans he raised objections to the involvement of the NZ Division. To this Wavell's responded that the New Zealand government had agreed to this and that he was not to discuss this with anyone other than Blamey. As a result Freyberg did not pass his concerns back to the New Zealand government because he felt it exceeded his authority. Blamey did not communicate his concerns onto the Australian government either, the following day limiting his response to a suggestion to Wavell that he take the matter up with the Australian government.

There the matter rested for several days. In the meantime Wavell flew to Athens with Churchill's foreign secretary, Anthony Eden, and the Chief of the Imperial General Staff, General Sir John Dill, on February 22 for further negotiations with Koryzis and Papagos. These turned out to be less than satisfactory, the Greeks still considering the size of the proposed force inadequate, though they eventually agreed to accept it. The British, however, objected to the Greek proposal to continue to hold on to the Albanian front and the Metaxas Line along the Bulgarian border, preferring one that ran along the northern slopes of Mount Olympus and the Vermion range. By the time Wavell's delegation left Athens, they thought they had obtained an agreement to defend this line. The Greeks, however, saw this as conditional on the British securing support of both Turkey and Yugoslavia.

Thus, it was not after Wavell, Eden and Dill had returned to Cairo from Athens that actual approaches to both the Australian and New Zealand governments were made, this being on February 25. The New Zealand government were happy to agree to the use of their division in Greece on the basis that Freyberg approved of this venture, their only stipulation being that it be fully equipped and accompanied by an armoured brigade. Getting approval from the Australian government, however, proved to be somewhat more complicated thanks to the fact that Menzies was now engaged in meetings with the British Government in London. The Australian War Cabinet decided that they needed to consult with Menzies, while the secretary for the Department of Defence, Frederick Sheldon, after learning of the opinion of Vice Admiral Thomas Phillips, the Vice Chief of the British Naval Staff, that the Greek expedition would end in evacuation, wanted to consult with Blamey. Unfortunately, Blamey was of no help, a cable received from him that same day only voicing his concerns over who was to lead this expeditionary force. This led to the belief that Blamey was happy with the venture and to the British receiving the required approval for the deployment of Australian troops. In part, too, both governments' approval was based on the strength of the British argument of the need to defend the Greeks against Axis aggression and on the British confidence in being able to persuade the Yugoslav and Turkish governments to join in the venture.

As it turned out, though Blamey had had genuine concerns about the whole venture, he was more focussed over the decision for the command of this force to go to British General Henry Maitland Wilson, arguing instead that it should have been himself because the bulk of the fighting troops came from Australia. This was not well received by Wavell who countered by stating that the Australian element was only one third of the total force committed, though where his figure came from was not clear. Nevertheless, Wavell could not be moved on this point and his choice of commander remained. Eventually Blamey did cable the Australian Minister for the Army, expressing his view that 'Military operation extremely hazardous in view of the disparity of opposing forces in number and training', but by this time it was March 9 and too late to stop the movement of forces to Greece.

In the meantime when Eden and Dill returned to Athens on March 2 they were unhappy to learn that Greek troops were still in place in Albania and on the Metaxas Line. The Greeks, for their part, were not pleased to learn of the failure of the British to secure support from Turkey and Yugoslavia. Unfortunately, as the British had found, this in part lay with the decrepit state of both the Turkish and Yugoslav armed forces but both nations had other issues. For the Turkish government it lay with their concerns that such an alliance could trigger an invasion through the Caucasus by their longstanding enemy, the Soviet Union, still an ally of Germany. As for the Yugoslavs, they were in the process of being courted by Germany to join the Axis, though this would only become apparent later.

In the end, a compromise was agreed whereby the British expeditionary force, known as W Force (after its commander Wilson), would occupy the line of the Aliákmon river, which runs north-east between the Vermion range and Mount Olympus to the Aegean Sea, to which the Greeks would divert some units, destined for the Metaxas Line. Nevertheless, the failure to obtain Turkish or Yugoslav support did lead to the British to re-evaluate the entire venture, with mixed results. While Admiral Andrew Cunningham, Commander-in-Chief of the Mediterranean Fleet, was confident he could protect the convoys travelling to Greece, Air Chief Marshall Longmore expressed grave concerns about his ability to deal with the German air force. At least General Dill, the Chief of the Imperial General Staff, and General Wavell were in agreement that it should be possible to extricate the force if it proved necessary. The evidence of German armour landing in Tripoli in mid-February was also disturbing, all this leading Churchill to wonder if the emphasis should be switched back to Libya. Unfortunately, by that stage the movement of W Force to Greece had already begun and so they resolved to continue with the operation.

OPERATION 'MARITA'

GERMAN PLANS TO invade Greece can be traced back to November 1940. Adolf Hitler, the Chancellor of Germany, primarily saw it as a way to secure his southern flank before his projected invasion of Russia. Some of it also related to concerns he had over Russia's intentions in the Balkans, particularly after Russia had forced Romania to hand over part of its territory. As originally conceived, German plans called for an operation to take over the northern Aegean littoral region, including the strategic port of Salonika (now Thessaloniki), the first stage of it being the occupation of Romania.

The situation changed after the British occupation of Crete because it brought British bombers within range of the Romanian oilfields. Worried by this, Hitler ordered the Oberkommando der Wehrmacht (OKW, Armed Forces High Command) to draw up plans for Operation 'Marita', the invasion of Greek Macedonia from Romania via Bulgaria. The OKW proposed deploying four divisions, though Hitler later increased this by another six. That same month Hitler made overtures to the Yugoslav government with the view to drawing them into the Axis, as control of the Belgrade–Nis–Salonika railway line was not only critical for 'Marita' but also for the redeployment of his forces for the forthcoming invasion of the Soviet Union. He initially approached the Yugoslav Foreign Minister, Lazar Cincar-Marković, on November 28 but this went nowhere. Nor did he have any more success on February 14, 1941, when a further meeting was held between himself, his Foreign Minister, Joachim von Ribbentrop, the Yugoslav Premier, Dragisha Cvetković, and Cincar-Marković. Hitler then upgraded Operation 'Marita' to a full invasion following the arrival of British troops in Greece at the beginning of March. Further discussion with Yugoslavia's Prince Regent Paul to Germany on March 4 also failed but then, suddenly, on March 18 the Yugoslav government agreed to join the Axis. This arrangement only lasted until March 26/27 when it was overthrown in a military coup d'état. Though the new leaders promised to remain friendly to Germany, Hitler was not convinced, instead ordering a full-scale invasion of Yugoslavia, Operation 'Strafgericht' (Punishment), initially to be launched on the second or third day of April. As the name suggested this was not simply an operation intended to take over the country but to exact revenge for what Hitler saw as their betrayal of his trust. This pushed the launch date of 'Marita' back a few days, the new date to be April 6.

This joint operation was entrusted to two armies. Yugoslavia was to be attacked by the 2. Armee under General der Kavallerie Maximilian von

To supervise the invasion of Yugoslavia and Greece, Hitler and the Oberkommando der Wehrmacht (OKW, German Armed Forces High Command) moved their headquarters closer to the battlefield. On April 12, Hitler's Sonderzug (special train) *Amerika* arrived at the little station of Mönichskirchen in Austria, some 70 kilometres from the Yugoslav border. Here it remained as Führerhauptquartier 'Frühlingssturm' (Spring Storm) for the next 14 days, until April 26, by which time his forces had conquered Yugoslavia and achieved the upper hand in Greece. On his arrival, Hitler inspected the guard of honour with (L-R) Generalfeldmarschall Wilhelm Keitel, chief of the OKW; Generalfeldmarschall Walther von Brauchitsch, C-in-C of the Army; Grossadmiral Erich Reader, C-in-C of the Kriegsmarine, and Reichsmarschall Hermann Göring, C-in-C of the Luftwaffe. (NIOD)

Weichs, while the 12. Armee under Generalfeldmarschall Wilhelm List was to invade Greece. In the case of 'Marita' the Germans were hoping to take advantage of the Greek preoccupation with their commitment in Albania to be unable to have sufficient troops to defend their borders with Yugoslavia and Bulgaria. For this operation the XXXX. Armee-Korps, commanded by General der Kavallerie Georg Stumme, was to thrust through southern Yugoslavia to Skopje and then south to the Monastir gap, which gave access

to Greece. At the same time the XXX. Armee-Korps, led by Generalleutnant Eugen Ott, and the mountain divisions of the XVIII. Gebirgs-Korps under General der Infanterie Franz Böhme (the 5. Gebirgs-Division under General der Gebirgstruppen Julius Ringel and the 6. Gebirgs-Division under Generalmajor Ferdinand Schörner) were to overcome the Metaxas Line, while the 2. Panzer-Division under Generalmajor Rudolf Veiel was to strike through southern Yugoslavia before swinging south into Greece to take Salonika. Thereafter all three corps were to converge on Salonika and drive south towards Athens. Air support was to be provided by the fighters, dive-bombers, bombers and transport aircraft of the VIII. Fliegerkorps under Generalfeldmarschall Wolfram Freiherr von Richthofen.

The small station remains virtually unchanged, a peaceful spot midst a wooded valley 70 kilometres south of Vienna. (Karel Margry)

OPERATION 'LUSTRE'

UNFORTUNATELY FOR GENERAL WILSON the British plans for the defence of Greece began to unravel as soon as the first elements of W Force reached the country, a movement carried out under the code-name Operation 'Lustre'. Being predicated on an Axis attack through Bulgaria not Yugoslavia, they were a compromise between the Greek desire to hold their frontier positions and the British wish for something more defensible along the mountain ranges to the south. This called for W Force to occupy a line along the Vermion range from Edessa to the Verria Pass, before following along the line of the Aliákmon river to the Aegean sea. After being shipped over early

Three of the principal Allied commanders in Greece were (L-R) Lieutenant-General Thomas Blamey (Australian Imperial Force), General Henry Maitland Wilson (W Force) and Major-General Bernard Freyberg (New Zealand Division). On April 12, changes in the command structure saw the formation of the Anzac Corps, an umbrella force that included the 6th Australian Division and the New Zealand Division, command of which fell to Blamey.
(ATL DA-14656)

in March, the British 1st Armoured Brigade was sent north, the bulk of it to hold the Edessa Pass. The problem with this was that it left it exposed to a possible outflanking by a German thrust through the Monastir gap, if the Germans did not respect Yugoslav neutrality or the Yugoslav army collapsed quickly. So to cover that, the 3rd Royal Tank Regiment was held back in reserve back at Amyntaio.

Over the next month the various components of the New Zealand Division were transported over, albeit interrupted for a time by the battle between British and Italian naval fleets south of Cape Matapan. The first to arrive was the 4th NZ Brigade (Brigadier Edward Puttick), which moved onto a heavily wooded ridge south of the Aliákmon river. To their right was the Greek 19th Mechanised Division (Major-General Nikolaos Lioumbas) on the open plains of the coastal sector behind an anti-tank ditch, still under construction. Next to arrive was the 6th NZ Brigade (Brigadier Harold Barrowclough), which was also deployed on the Aliákmon plain. Towards the end of the month the last infantry unit, the 5th NZ Brigade (Brigadier James Hargest), reached Greece, the divisional artillery units arriving around the same time. Thus by the time of the German invasion the entire New Zealand Division had reached Greece.

The Australians were slower to arrive. Wavell had originally wanted Lavarack's 7th Australian Division to go first as it was then based in Egypt. This was to be followed by the 6th Australian Division in Cyrenaica, after it had been replaced by the 9th Australian Division from Palestine. This move was supported by Blamey's Chief-of-Staff, Brigadier Sydney Rowell. Blamey, however, insisted that the 6th Australian Division should go first, arguing that they had had the benefit of combat experience, though there were views among some Australians that Blamey's long-term dislike of Lavarack also had something to do with it. This impasse continued until early March, Blamey finding out that Wavell's plan was still in place on the 5th. At this point he insisted that the order of the despatch of the two divisions be reversed, to which Wavell finally agreed. Wavell, however, was still not willing to release any units from the 6th Australian Division until an equivalent was brought in to replace it. This ultimately resulted in a complicated process whereby a brigade was detached from the 9th Australian Division in Palestine to replace a brigade from the 7th Australian Division in Egypt, which was then sent forward to Cyrenaica. Only then could a brigade from the 6th Australian Division be released for dispatch to Greece. The effect of this was to considerably delay the shipment of Australian units to Greece, the 16th Australian Brigade (Brigadier Arthur Allen) being the first to reach the country on March 19. Even then, this was only after the brigade found itself held up for three days in Mersa Matruh by a severe dust storm, thereafter taking eight days to reach their staging camp. Once in Greece, they were directed north to hold the Verria Pass in the Vermion range. The next Australian units to arrive, among them two infantry battalions, two artillery regiments and their anti-tank regiment,

An unknown photographer captured men from the carrier platoon of the 25th NZ Battalion traveling by train on their way north to the Aliákmon Line on March 21. Little did they realise that they were passing through the Pineios gorge, the site of what would prove to be a critical battle covering their very retreat four weeks later. (ATL DA-08170-F)

did not reach Greece until literally three days before the Germans launched 'Marita', the infantry being rushed up to join the British 1st Armoured Brigade at the Edessa Pass. Unfortunately, the last infantry units from the division, the battalions of the 17th Australian Brigade and the 2/11th Battalion, did not arrive until April 12, by which time the German invasion was well under way.

That was only the beginning of their problems. General Freyberg, the commander of the New Zealand Division, was disturbed to discover that the Greek 19th Mechanised Division was little more than a motorised brigade, resulting in the Greeks being sent north into the Axios valley and Doiran gap. In their place Freyberg extended the front of his division, moving the 6th NZ Brigade into the gap left in the coastal sector by the departing Greeks, while placing the 5th NZ Brigade in reserve at the Olympus Pass.

Nevertheless, Freyberg still had misgivings over the deployment of his two forward brigades, holding the view that they should be withdrawn to the line of the Olympus mountains, an opinion shared by Blamey when he arrived in Greece on March 19. Blamey also had concerns about the Monastir gap and the possibility that the Germans might exploit this route if they decided to attack through Yugoslavia. However, Wilson would have none of this, his concerns partly driven by how the Greeks would regard such a withdrawal.

One final gap that needed to be filled was where the Olympus range met the Aegean Sea at the village of Neos Panteleimonas on Platamon ridge and where the Salonika to Athens railway line passed through a tunnel, half a kilometre long. Along with the Pineios river gorge, an eight-kilometre-long wooded gulch located immediately south of the tunnel with the railway on the north bank and a road on the south bank, this area – a natural defile – was strategically important because it controlled the eastern exit of the Tempi valley that linked the plain of Thessaly in the south with Macedonia in the north. Not that the Allied commanders were the first to recognise the importance of the area, as the Crusader castle on top of Platamon ridge testified to. According to Rowell, Blamey's Chief-of-Staff, everyone at Blamey's I Australian Corps Headquarters regarded this area as impregnable.

Orders for Brigadier Hargest, the 5th NZ Brigade commander, were to hold this with one company but to prepare the area for an entire battalion should circumstances require it. Thus, on the night of March 28/29, D Company of the 26th NZ Battalion reached Platamon ridge with orders to prepare positions for a company. However, after inspecting the area two days later, the division's GSO1 (Chief-of-Staff), Colonel Keith Stewart, asked that it be expanded to hold an entire battalion. This involved digging positions around the castle, another one covering it from the rear, with the line being extended up towards Point 266 above the village of Neos Panteleimonas. Freyberg inspected this work on April 4, with Hargest, and noted somewhat prophetically that 'if a battalion took it over, it would be expected to hold it for only 24 hours: by then reinforcements would have been sent up from Larissa'.

THE GERMANS INVADE GREECE

THE GERMANS OPENED their joint attacks on Yugoslavia and Greece on the morning of April 6. Within two days the mountain troops of General der Infanterie Böhme's XVIII. Gebirgs-Korps had overcome the Greeks in their mountain bunkers along the Metaxas Line, while the 2. Panzer-Division had slipped around behind the line, an Ultra decrypt of intercepted German radio traffic (OL 52) stating their goal was Salonika. After reaching Strumica that evening the division continued its advance over the next two days,

The German invasion of Greece – Operation 'Marita' – began on April 6 with a direct assault on the Metaxas Line on the border between Greece and Bulgaria by German mountain troops. Meanwhile, the 2. Panzer-Division launched a sweeping westward drive through Yugoslavia, followed by a southward turn into Greece towards the port city of Salonika. Here a PzKpfw III from the division's Panzer-Regiment 3 negotiates a partially-destroyed bridge near the town of Kilkis, located halfway between the border and Salonika, on April 9. (USNA StM 141-33)

The Germans have made the broken span negotiable with pieces of bridging equipment. Panzer-Regiment 3 started the Greek campaign with a strength of 116 tanks: 45 PzKpfw IIs, 51 PzKpfw IIIs and 20 PzKpfw IVs. (USNA StM 141-34)

negotiating muddy, rain-soaked roads and damaged bridges. On April 8 it overran the Greek 19th Mechanised Division at Lake Doiran and entered the port town of Salonika on the morning of April 9.

From the point of view of W Force the timing could not have been worse. General Wilson had just been informed that the 7th Australian Division was not coming to Greece thanks to the invasion of Cyrenaica by the Afrika-Korps. The German invasion of Yugoslavia also signalled to Wilson the possibility of a German thrust through the Monastir gap. Accordingly, the British 1st Armoured Brigade was pulled back from Edessa on the night of April 8/9, with orders to hold the Kleidi Pass, the brigade's motor battalion, the 1st Rangers (King's Royal Rifle Corps), taking over defence of the pass itself, while the 3rd Royal Tanks took over a position further back at Sotir. Command of this ad hoc group was given to Major-General Mackay, the 6th Australian Division commander, acquiring the name Mackay Force in the process. Additional support came from the Greek Dodecanese Regiment to the north of Lake Vegorritis and the Greek Cavalry Regiment at Florina. Early on the morning of April 9 Mackay Force was joined by the 2/4th Battalion from the 19th Australian Brigade (Brigadier George Vasey) that had just been relieved of guard duties at Larissa on April 5. The battalion took up positions to the left of the pass. The last unit to arrive was the 2/8th Battalion, also from the 19th Brigade, on the night of April 9, a journey north that had started in Athens on April 6.

Holding the Kleidi Pass was also critical to a redeployment of W Force to a new defensive line that ran along the Aliákmon river inland to its junction with the Venetikos river. Under this new plan the New Zealand Division, now under Blamey's command, was to be pulled back from the Aliákmon plain. Blamey's first order was for the 4th NZ Brigade to take over the defence of the Servia Pass, located west of the Olympus Pass, the brigade moving out from their positions early on the morning of April 9. Later, on the night of April 9/10, the 6th NZ Brigade began to withdraw back through the Olympus Pass to reserve positions south of Elasson to cover the road to Larissa, leaving behind the Divisional Cavalry Regiment along the south bank of the Aliákmon. The final move in this reshuffle saw the 16th Australian Brigade withdraw from the Verria Pass on the night of April 10/11, finally crossing the Aliákmon on April 13, to take up positions to the right of the 4th NZ Brigade above Servia. The following day Blamey announced that his I Australian

Salonika, 50 kilometres further to the south, was entered unopposed by the division later that morning. Bildberichter (war photographer) Walter Dick from Propaganda-Kompanie 690 pictured a PzKpfw III from Panzer-Regiment 3 passing through the city. (BA Bild 101I-162-0257-09)

Corps, which now included the New Zealand Division, had been renamed the Anzac Corps.

April 9 also saw the deployment of the 21st NZ Battalion (Lieutenant-Colonel Neil Macky) on Platamon ridge from reserve positions at Athens where they had been under the command of 80 Base Sub-Area. Macky's original orders had been for the battalion to proceed to Katerini, only to be told on reaching Larissa of their new assignment. The rest of their journey was mostly smooth, interrupted only once when the Greek train crew stopped the train and abandoned it on sighting a running air battle overhead. Once at Platamon, A Company (Captain Robert McClymont) took over the right flank by the Crusader castle, while B Company (Major Clement Le Lievre), to their left, began occupying positions forward of Point 266. C Company (Captain Walter Tongue) was given responsibility for holding the village of Palaios Panteleimonas a kilometre distant further up the hills, while D Company (Captain Archibald Trousdale) was placed in reserve. The Carrier Platoon remained back near Platamon railway station, where they had unloaded the carriers. From there they maintained patrols

Salonika is today known as Thessaloniki and the panzer was passing the Hamza Bey Mosque on Egnatia Street. The building is currently under restoration after being handed back to the city authorities. Prior to that it had served as a restaurant. (Jeffrey Plowman)

along the beach from the railway tunnel to the northernmost channel of the Pineios river delta.

That night around midnight, their artillery support – A Troop, 27th Battery, 5th NZ Field Regiment under Lieutenant Lawrence Williams – finally reached Platamon from Katerini, having had to manhandle their 25-pounder guns over some rough country towards the end of their journey and then winch them over a stream because the bridge was too weak to take them. They set up the guns among some willows 500 metres to the south of Platamon station, establishing an OP position for Williams in front of the castle, above the railway tunnel on the seaward side.

On April 10 Macky's battalion was joined by a wireless detachment from A Troop, NZ Signals, consisting of signalmen Lance-Sergeant George Laurie and Staff-Sergeant Herbert Leary, with a No. 11 wireless set and a spare set of batteries. Accompanying them was Lance-Corporal Kenneth 'Bully' Hayes, with a No. 9 remote control unit, he being tasked with establishing communication with Freyberg's Advanced Divisional Headquarters on the permanent line running along the railway line. The signallers travelled down by train because a reconnaissance earlier by Captain Charles Pryor from Divisional Signals had been unable to find a vehicular approach to the castle, considering the track only fit for horse-drawn vehicles and negotiable, with care, by an 8-cwt truck, its muddy surface becoming quite impassable for wheeled vehicles in wet weather.

The following day, an engineer detail – No. 1 Section, 19th (Army Troops) Company, NZE under Lieutenant Frederick Jones – arrived. They had only one-fifth of the explosives necessary for a proper job, nor the tools either, but did have a large naval mine, one of many purchased by Lieutenant-Colonel George Clifton, the divisional CRE (Commander Royal Engineers), when the division was still in Egypt. In addition they had a quantity of anti-tank mines. The 7th NZ Field Company had decided not to return these and other demolition equipment to the British Army before leaving England with the rest of the division's 2nd Echelon in January 1941, sharing them with the other engineer units before all departed for Greece in April. What Jones' men did lack was a compressor and pneumatic drills, so they were forced to use pick-axes to drive holes in the concrete sides of the railway tunnel. Charges were also laid under the rails at both ends of the tunnel and along the saddle track. The anti-tank mines they laid on forward slopes near the top of the ridge. While they were doing this, 2nd Lieutenant Bill Southworth, the commander of No. 7 Platoon of A Company, persuaded them to give him a few sticks of explosives (with detonators and safety fuses attached) after telling them that the battalion had not been supplied with any hand-grenades.

FIRST ENCOUNTERS (April 9-13)

ON APRIL 9, the fourth day of Operation 'Marita', leading elements of General Stumme's XXXX. Armee-Korps entered Greece, the Schützen-Brigade 'Leibstandarte-SS Adolf Hitler' (LSSAH) reaching the town of Florina later that day. However, when they tried to push onto the Kleidi Pass they came under fire from Mackay Force and were forced to fall back. In some ways the timing could not have been worse for Mackay Force. The following evening the 2/8th Australian Battalion had only just completed their climb up to the

The panzer division's next obstacle in its southward drive was the Aliákmon river. By the time advance elements reached the river on the afternoon of April 12, both brigades of the New Zealand Division had withdrawn, leaving only the NZ Divisional Cavalry (with 28 armoured cars and 44 carriers) holding the river line at Niselli. Three days earlier, No. 3 Section of the 6th Field Company, NZE had blown the bridges there, the first one to go being the railway bridge. Corporal Stratton Morrin from the Divisional Cavalry carried a camera and photographed the results of their handiwork. (Stratton Morrin)

The bridge was repaired and kept in use for another four decades, eventually being abandoned in 1998 when the new double-track Athens to Thessaloniki line was opened. George Handrinos pictured the disused span in 2000. (George Handrinos)

The road bridge, upstream from the railway bridge, had also been destroyed by No. 3 Section on April 9 but this did not deter some motorcycle combinations from Kradschützen-Bataillon 2, the motorcycle-borne infantry battalion and vanguard of the 2. Panzer-Division, from riding up to it on April 12. They were promptly shot up, only one escaping. (ATL DA-12666)

The remains of the old road bridge can still be seen today. Following the successful conclusion of Operation 'Marita', the Germans rebuilt most road and rail bridges that had been destroyed in the campaign. However, they in turn systematically destroyed all important bridges when they pulled out of Greece in December 1944, which suggests that they were in fact responsible for the demolition seen here. (Nikos Valasiadis)

ridge and were in the process of digging in when they came under attack from patrols from the LSSAH.

Initially, things went well for Mackay Force, an Ultra signal (OL 2042) on April 11 reporting that the LSSAH was meeting violent resistance. However, the arrival of the 9. Panzer-Division (Generalleutnant Alfred von Hubkicki) on the afternoon of April 12 finally saw the tables turn against Mackay Force, forcing the 1st Rangers out of the pass. That night the Australians finally abandoned their positions on the ridges on either side of the pass, the withdrawal of the 2/8th Australian Battalion turning into a rout, with many men abandoning their weapons as they ran back. Their remnants were evacuated by trucks to Servia.

To the east the attack on the New Zealand positions developed more slowly due to German logistical failures. Panzer-Regiment 3 (Oberst Hermann Balck) and the bulk of Panzer-Aufklärungs-Abteilung 5 (Major Schmiedmann) from Generalleutnant Veiel's 2. Panzer-Division ended up grounded at Chalkidona, outside Salonika, there being only fuel for their tanks for a few kilometres. More was expected within 48 hours but did not even arrive then. What available fuel they had was issued to Panzer-Aufklärungs-Abteilung 5 to enable them to send reconnaissance patrols towards Edessa, Verria and south to Yidha on April 12. General Böhme, the XVIII. Gebirgs-Korps commander, also ordered the 6. Gebirgs-Division south toward Verria but their advance in that direction became unnecessary when reports were received at 2.40 p.m. that it was free of the enemy. In fact aerial reconnaissance early in the afternoon had noted heavy traffic on the Ptolemais road; most probably elements of the 16th Australian Brigade pulling back to Servia.

Orders were also issued to Schützen-Regiment 2, accompanied by elements of Panzer-Aufklärungs-Abteilung 5 and the five PzKpfw IIs from the light tank platoon of the 2. Kompanie of the I. Abteilung of Panzer-Regiment 3, to conduct a reconnaissance in force towards the Aliákmon river. Intelligence reports had indicated that the area south of the river was being held by two New Zealand divisions with around 200 tanks. In

Kradschützen-Bataillon 2 made several more attempts against the Divisional Cavalry by the road bridge on April 13, all of which were easily repulsed. They then turned their attention to the railway bridge further downstream, which forced the New Zealanders to start a staged withdrawal from the river. The subsequent German crossing in rubber boats, seen here, was unopposed. (Franz Steinzer)

With the south bank of the Aliákmon secure, the 2. Panzer-Division was able to move over heavier equipment by way of a pontoon ferry assembled by Panzer-Pionier-Bataillon 38. Here a PzKpfw II and some motorcycle combinations make the crossing. (USNA StM 142-03)

The distinctive line of hills in the distance, seen from the south side of the river, confirms that the ferry was located downstream of the current road bridge at Niselli. (Google)

actual fact the only force there was the NZ Divisional Cavalry Regiment, its A Squadron occupying a stretch of the river from the village of Aiynion to the main bridge, while B Squadron covered the riverbank further upstream. With them were O Troop of the 7th NZ Anti-Tank Regiment, E Troop of the 5th NZ Field Regiment and No. 3 Section of the 5th NZ Field Company.

Unaware of the true nature of the defences along the Aliákmon river the Germans continued south until at 1.06 p.m. on the afternoon of April 12 one of their motorcycle patrols reported that they had come under fire from the direction of the river near Niselli. According to New Zealand reports around 2 p.m., led by motorcycle and sidecar combinations, the Germans reached the site of the blown road bridge. The Divisional Cavalry troop by the bridge opened up, killing all the motorcyclists, save for one who escaped. After this the Germans limited themselves to sniping at the New Zealand positions,

Among the vehicles ferried over the river was this PzKpfw II, most probably from the leichter Panzerzug (light tank platoon) of the I. Abteilung of Panzer-Regiment 3. Oberst Hermann Balck, the regimental commander, had lent this platoon to the attacking force and they remained with them, at least, until they reached the Greek anti-tank ditch south of Katerini on April 14 where they again encountered the NZ Divisional Cavalry. (USNA StM 142-02)

The main force of Panzer-Regiment 3 reached the Aliákmon river at 7.25 a.m. on April 15, by which time the ferry there had been replaced by a wooden trestle bridge suitable for heavier vehicles such as these PzKpfw IVs. The divisional engineers had also built a corduroy road connecting the bridge with the main road between Niselli and Katerini to improve the tanks' passage over the soggy ground by the river. (Stefano di Giusto)

More vehicles being transported over: a SdKfz 10 half-track, which appears to be fitted with bridging equipment, a PzKpfw I and a motorcycle combination. (USNA StM 141-37)

then pulled back. That evening they called for additional support, including at least an additional company of anti-tank guns.

The following morning (April 13), German infantry came forward and launched assault boats simultaneously upstream and downstream of the road bridge at which point the emplaced cavalrymen opened up at point-blank range. No assault troops survived this barrage of fire; nor

when the attack was repeated three or four times, the 25-pounder guns of E Troop joining in on those occasions. As the morning wore on, German armoured half-tracks were seen approaching with more infantry, two of these being destroyed by artillery at over 9,000 yards' range. The Germans then switched their attention to a demolished railway bridge downstream. At this point the Divisional Cavalry began a phased withdrawal, starting with B Squadron, followed by their supporting artillery around midday. The other two cavalry squadrons began to pull out later that afternoon, all assembling at a Greek-constructed anti-tank ditch further back. This enabled Schützen-Regiment 2 to establish a bridgehead over the river at Niselli around 6 p.m. that evening, but too late to continue the advance that day.

That same day, April 13, the British 1st Armoured Brigade withdrew from their rearguard position at Sotir and, after a brief engagement at dusk with the 9. Panzer-Division at Ptolemais, fell back through Kozani, re-assembling south of the Aliákmon river. Luckily for the British, lack of fuel for Hubkicki's tanks prevented them from following up. However, the brigade was now in serious trouble, its main strike element, the 3rd Royal Tanks, having lost so many of its A10 Cruiser tanks, from mechanical failure, that it had been reduced to the size of a squadron. Worse still, with

While the NZ Divisional Cavalry were facing elements of the 2. Panzer-Division along the Aliákmon river, 90 kilometres further to the north-west the 3rd Royal Tank Regiment, part of the British 1st Armoured Brigade, covered the retreat of Mackay Force at the Kleidi Pass by blocking the advance of the 9. Panzer-Division, first at Sotir and then later at Komanos, to the north of Ptolemais, before withdrawing through Kozani and over the Aliákmon river. Covering this final stage was Lieutenant Robert Crisp's A10 Cruiser tank *Cool* (T-5946) from No. 9 Troop of C Squadron. It had to be abandoned north of Kozani due to a broken fuel pump on April 14. The fate of the 3rd Royal Tanks in the Greek campaign was singularly unfortunate. They had arrived in Greece with 52 A10s, most of which were in poor mechanical shape, with badly worn tracks. They gave a good account of themselves, claiming six panzers knocked out on April 13, but in the course of one week (April 11-18) they lost all their tanks, 51 to mechanical problems (track breakages, steering failures, engine failures, etc) and only one to enemy action. (Robert Gregory Collection)

The hills in the background, among them Mount Skopou on the left, provide a perfect match, placing *Cool* some 12 kilometres north of Kozani on the main road to Ptolemais. In his war memoirs *The Gods Were Neutral*, published in 1959, Crisp maintained that he turned the tank around and ordered the turret to be swung back over the engine deck to face north but this view is taken looking towards the south-east, meaning that the whole tank was actually facing northwards. (Google)

On the night of April 10/11, covered by Mackay Force at the Kleidi Pass, the battalions of the 16th Australian Brigade began to pull out of their positions at the Verria Pass. Having made their way over the mountain range seen in the distance these troops from the 2/2nd Battalion are being ferried over the Aliákmon on April 13. (AWM 007848)

The drowning of the Aliákmon under the waters of the Polyphytos reservoir in the Kozani prefecture makes it impossible to get close to the former course of the river today. However, the ridgeline on the horizon allows us to pinpoint the spot where the Australians crossed to a place near the town of Velvento. (Google)

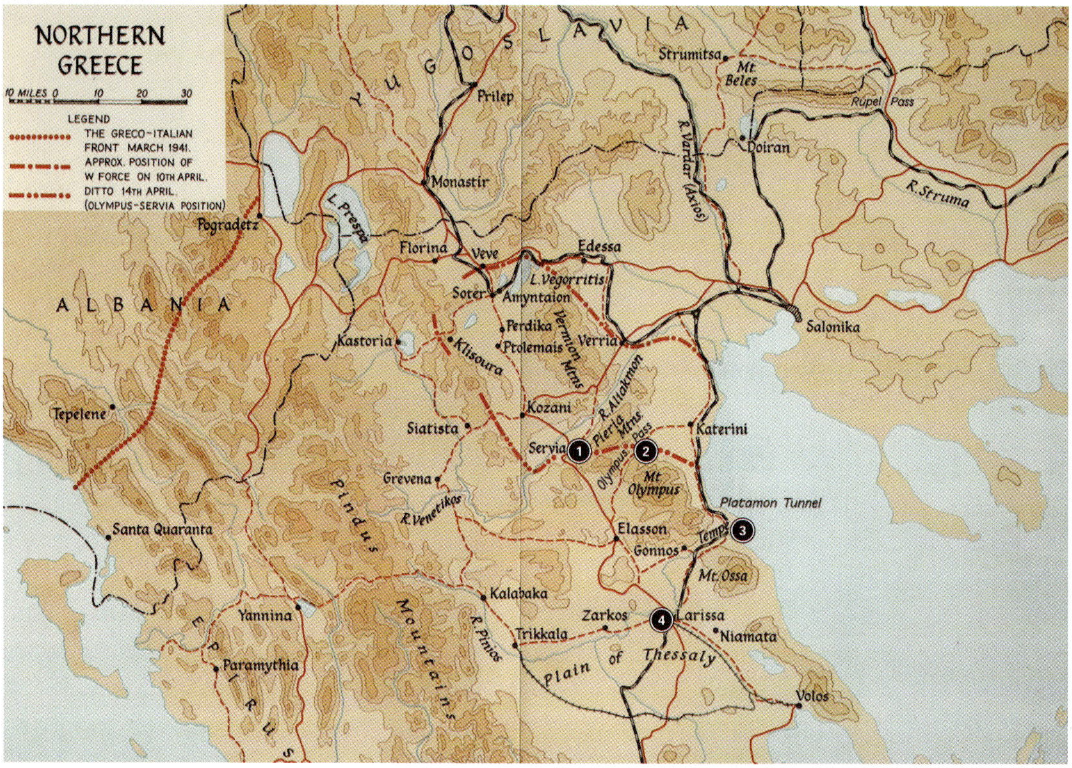

After withdrawing from the Aliákmon Line, the Anzac troops occupied a more-defensible position along the Olympus mountain range and the Venetikos river, the New Zealand Division taking over responsibility for the Servia [1] and Olympus [2] Passes. The coastal route via Platamon and the Pineios river gorge [3] – better known from ancient times as the Vale of Tempe – to Larissa [4] was considered of lesser importance. In the eyes of the Anzac commanders, the Platamon gap offered only a minor threat as the only passage it gave to the south was by way of a rough track over the Platamon ridge and a railway tunnel beneath the ridge on the coast, and both of these led to the equally difficult passage of the Pineios gorge. (British Official History)

the main road from Kozani to Servia reserved for the Australians, the brigade was directed onto the secondary road from Kozani to Grevena, a move that led to more losses from their mechanically compromised cruiser tanks.

This move, coupled with disturbing news that the Greeks were struggling to conform with the withdrawal of Mackay Force, exposed a serious hole in the Anzac Corps defence, that of an attack through Kalabaka to Trikkala and one that threatened to cut off Anzac troops north of Larissa. On April 14, to counter this, Lieutenant-General Blamey ordered the commander of the newly-arrived 17th Australian Brigade, Brigadier Stanley Savige, to establish a new ad hoc force, Savige Force, and use it to secure this open left flank. Thus, around 3 p.m., Savige set off for Kalabaka, via Trikkala, with his own Brigade Carrier Platoon and the seven A13 Cruiser tanks from Headquarters Squadron of the British 1st Armoured Brigade. Two hours later, they were joined by the 2/11th Australian Battalion (from the 19th Australian Brigade) and the bulk of the 2/5th Australian Battalion (from Savige's own brigade), along with a battery from the 2/1st Australian Anti-Tank Regiment.

DESCENT INTO CHAOS (April 14-15)

ON APRIL 14, Schützen-Regiment 2 (Oberst Hans Koelitz) caught up with the NZ Divisional Cavalry at the Greek anti-tank ditch on the open coastal plains south of the Aliákmon. Here they were held for two hours before the New Zealanders finally pulled back behind the 5th NZ Brigade at the Olympus Pass. Their road now clear, the Germans struck south, entering Katerini at 3 p.m. The way was now open for the 2. Panzer-Division to push on to Larissa, once it could be assembled into a coherent formation. However, it was still quite scattered, its Schützen-Regiment 304 having only recently departed from Salonika, while Panzer-Regiment 3 was still on its way south towards Niselli, with only Schützen-Regiment 2 in Katerini itself. Unfortunately, forward movement of these units was heavily constrained by numerous demolitions along the main axis of advance. That left Generalleutnant Veiel few options other than to order the division's motorcycle unit, Kradschützen-Bataillon 2 (Oberstleutnant Carl Stollbrock), to reconnoitre the coastal road as far as Panteleimonas.

At the same time as the Germans entered Katerini, Freyberg paid a final visit to the 21st Battalion on Platamon ridge. He informed Lieutenant-Colonel Macky of General Wilson's plans to withdraw to a line across the Greek peninsula at Thermopylae, 150 kilometres further south, and of how important it was to deny Platamon ridge and the coast road to the enemy. He left Macky with the assurance that, because of the nature of the terrain, they were only likely to encounter infantry. So it was that around 6.30 p.m. a puff of dust on the main road resolved itself into a light tank and some motorcyclists who dismounted 1,500 metres away to survey the New Zealand positions with binoculars. With a quick burst of Bren gun fire the German party fell over themselves in their haste to get away. However, unseen by the New Zealand infantry, some elements managed to sneak further forward, Lieutenant Williams, from his artillery observation post above the railway tunnel, observing what he described as 'some German recce vehicles – probably armoured and larger than Bren carriers – make their way unobserved almost up to the tunnel. There they nosed around and then retired to the cover of an orchard a short distance back'. Not long after, a long line of traffic started to roll over the road and into some dead ground behind a rise, among it '30 vehicles AFVs troop tpt' – as reported in a radio message sent to Freyberg at 0.50 a.m. on April 15. These were soon targeted by the New Zealanders' mortar platoon, some trucks being

Responsibility for defence of the Platamon ridge, which lay forward of the town after which it was named, was assigned to the 21st NZ Battalion, supported by a troop of field guns and a section of engineers. No anti-tank guns were attached to the force as it was considered that the Germans would not send armour this way. This was the view looking north from the ridge. (ATL DA-10986)

Today this area is known as the Olympos Riviera, the Akti Platamona beach stretching north from beneath the ridge being the longest beach in Greece.
(Jeffrey Plowman)

set alight and screams and shouts of the Germans being audible in the distance.

At this point Macky ordered the engineers to blow the charges in the railway tunnel. The first attempt with 350lbs of explosive was only partially successful, a combination of insufficient charges and the fact that the cavities behind the concrete had absorbed some of the shock. A second charge of 50lbs of gelignite brought down most of the lining of the roof. The process was completed by setting off charges under the rails at either end of the tunnel. Nevertheless, the engineers were still unhappy with this, thinking that repairs would only take six hours. Nor were they satisfied with the craters blown in the saddle track. So in the early hours of April 15, when the 21st Battalion contacted Freyberg's headquarters to update them of the situation, they also informed them that the tunnel demolition had only been partially successful and put in a request for more explosives. This was passed on to Wilson at his advanced headquarters in a village just outside Elasson, who then contacted 81 Base Sub-Area. However, the request was never actioned. Unbeknown to Wilson, his Deputy Director of Supplies and Transport, Brigadier Wilfred d'Auvergne Collings, had ordered 81 Base Sub-Area to abandon Larissa and move back to Thebes. The move was already underway by that stage, with their workshop sections and heavy equipment on the road south, while the remainder of the activity there was directed towards moving base troops, ammunition and essential stores out by rail.

Nevertheless, reports of this initial encounter by the motorcyclists led Veiel to believe that the pass was lightly held and that the British were holding the castle area only, though there was little he could do immediately. With the road between Yidha and Katerini clogged with traffic, and the road itself in poor condition due to the demolitions and heavy rainfall, the forward movement of Panzer-Regiment 3 had to be put off till the following morning.

That night Veiel established two Kampfgruppen (combat groups), both with a mission to strike out for Larissa. One, under Oberst Koelitz, the commander of Schützen-Regiment 2, was to take the inland route via the Olympus Pass and Elasson, while the second under Oberst Balck, the commander of Panzer-Regiment 3, was to follow the line of advance from Panteleimonas on the coast via Platamon ridge towards the Pineios river gorge. For his battlegroup, Balck was assigned the I. Abteilung (Oberstleutnant Karl Decker) of his own Panzer-Regiment 3, the 2. Kompanie of Panzerjäger-Abteilung 38 and the 2. and 7. Batterien of Artillerie-Regiment 74; along with the I. Bataillon of Schützen-Regiment 304 (Oberst Hans-Ulrich Back) and Kradschützen-Bataillon 2, the latter already at Panteleimonas. (Later, the 7. Kompanie of the II. Bataillon of Schützen-Regiment 304 was added as well). Corps commander Böhme also sent the 6. Gebirgs-Division on a parallel course further to the west with the aim of passing over the south-eastern slopes of the Olympus range.

On the morning of April 15 Freyberg informed Anzac Corps HQ at Gerania of the situation at Platamon and asked them to assume responsibility for

Sitting on the ridge was Platamon Castle. Constructed by the Crusaders between 1204 and 1222, it was a natural defensive position with its commanding view of the valley to the north. Sergeant George Kaye, the New Zealand official photographer, pictured what are probably men from the 21st NZ Battalion at the keep. (They were not the first New Zealanders based in the area, D Company of the 26th Battalion having already been sent there on March 27 to build defence works.) (ATL DA-11836)

While the 21st NZ Battalion did not occupy the castle itself, the latter did suffer some damage in the resulting battle. The damage to the crenulations seen in the wartime picture apparently preceded the fighting and has now been repaired. Today, the keep is not accessible to the general public and most of the castle walls are unsafe to walk. (Jeffrey Plowman)

the 21st Battalion so that he could focus on the defence of the Servia and Olympus Passes. He also passed on to Corps HQ the radio traffic from the 21st Battalion from the previous night. According to Lieutenant-Colonel Clifton, the divisional CRE, these messages, at first thought to be bogus, gave the staff at Corps Headquarters 'one hell of a shock.' Nevertheless Lieutenant-General Blamey did nothing, considering Macky to be alarmist. Instead, he and Anzac Corps HQ continued to monitor their messages for the rest of the day as the situation at Platamon deteriorated further.

By the morning of April 15, from General Wilson's point of view, the situation in Greece had deteriorated considerably to the extent that more-drastic action was required. Notwithstanding the Greek plight on their left flank and the appearance of German troops at Platamon ridge, reports had been received of German troops attempting to launch a bridge over the Aliákmon river at Servia on the afternoon of April 14 and later losing a tank in the river in an attempt to cross it. This suggested that the line of the Venetikos and Aliákmon rivers, to which they had withdrawn, was no longer tenable and that the only option was to pull further back to a line running through Thermopylae. His fears may also have been strengthened later that day by the receipt of an Ultra intercept (OL 2067) at 0514 that the 2. Panzer-Division was to receive fighter protection between Katerini, Larissa and the Aegean coast from dawn onwards.

Whatever the case, this resulted in a flurry of orders that set in motion the speed-up of the withdrawal of the Anzac Corps. Among these was the establishment of a number of brigade-group sized blocking forces to cover this move. These involved the British 1st Armoured Brigade at Grevena, Savige Force at Kalabaka and the 6th NZ Brigade between Elasson and Tyrnavos. Wilson also took over control of the 2/6th and 2/7th Australian Battalions from the 17th Australian Brigade, at that stage still under orders to join Savige Force, with the view to using them to establish another blocking force south of Larissa at the passes over to Domokos and Lamia. As if to reinforce this change, that afternoon Wilson arrived at Kalabaka to inform Brigadier Savige that these two battalions and the rest of the 2/5th Battalion would not be coming but were required elsewhere. One unfortunate aspect to this raft of changes also occurred around this time. With Anzac Corps Headquarters having been given responsibility for the withdrawal, Brigadier Rowell said that: 'this was the last time Wilson's headquarters ever came "into the picture" as far as running the W Force campaign in Greece was concerned'.

Blamey added his own twist to this that evening when he sent out his orders for the phased disengagement of units from the Aliákmon Line, with orders for the New Zealand Division to hold the Servia and Olympus Passes to allow the 19th Australian Brigade and the 26th NZ Battalion to be withdrawn on the night of April 15/16 from the Servia Pass. After they were successfully clear 16th Australian Brigade was to pull out and establish a third blocking force at Zarkos, between Kalabaka and Larissa. In essence this established three blocking positions of brigade-group size facing a potential threat in the

The view looking west towards the village of Neos Panteleimonas from the vicinity of the castle.

B Company of the 21st NZ Battalion was placed on Point 266, the distinctive hill in the centre above Neos Panteleimonas, to cover the possibility that the Germans might try to cut off their retreat from the ridge using some of the tracks in the area. (There is some ambiguity over where Panteleimonas was located, there being Pallios Panteleimonas and Neos Panteleimonas close to each other. The New Zealand official histories clearly describe C Company as being at Pallios Panteleimonas, which is some 2.5 kilometres from Platamon Castle (it can just be seen in this image). However, it is not clear which village the German records refer to, though in some cases it is more likely to be Neos Panteleimonas.) (Jeffrey Plowman)

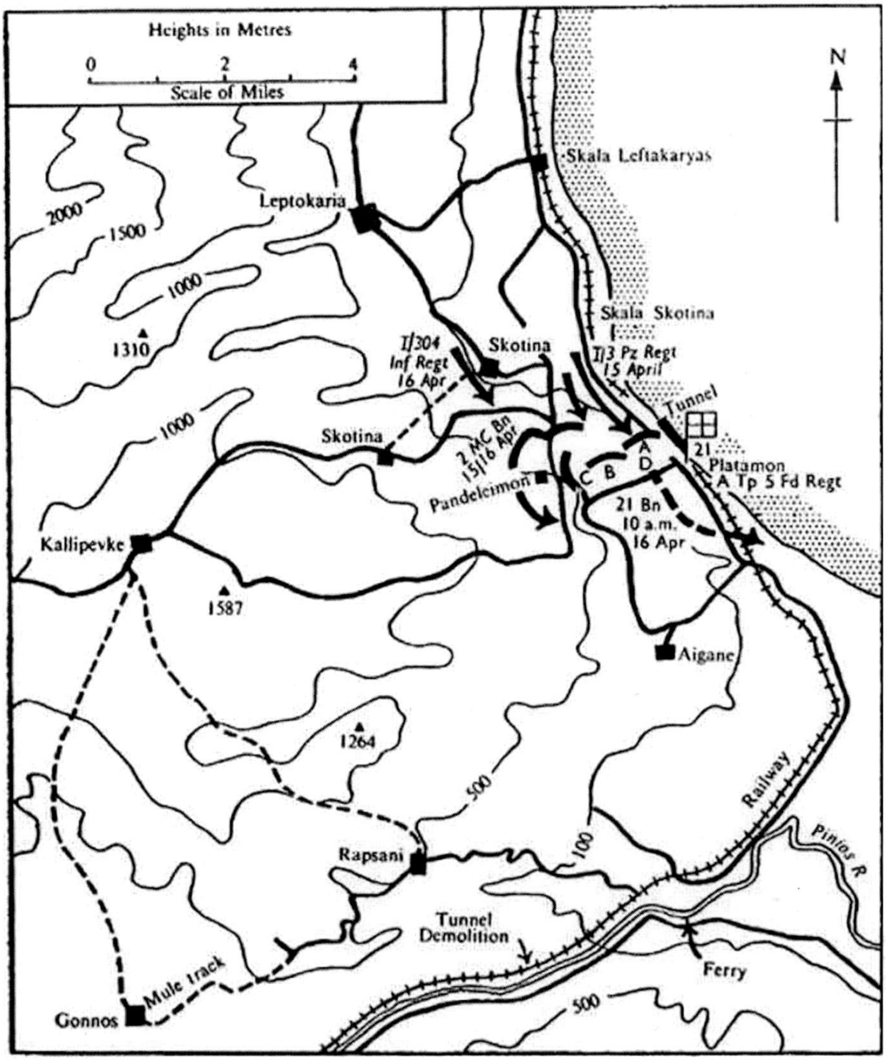

The advance elements of the 2. Panzer-Division's Kampfgruppe Balck reached Platamon ridge on April 14, launching their first attack the next day. The 21st NZ Battalion managed to hold the position until the morning of April 16, when they were forced to abandon it and pull back to the Pineios gorge. (New Zealand Official History)

west, leaving a single battalion group in the east – the 21st NZ Battalion at Platamon – to deal with a genuine incursion.

As it so happened, setting up the final blocking force to the south of Larissa was not without its problems. Both of the assigned battalions had just spent April 14 facing constant interruptions on the journey to Domokos from Athens as their Greek train crews stopped and abandoned their engine every time they saw an aircraft in the sky. For the 2/7th Australian Battalion and D Company, 2/5th Australian Battalion, there was to be more of this on the 15th. Not so for their sister unit, the 2/6th Australian Battalion. After setting off from Domokos they were intercepted at Pharsala and sent back to Domokos. However, the 2/7th Australian Battalion, having departed half an hour earlier, managed to pass through Pharsala unchallenged, only to spend the next 18 hours on the train. This included a two-hour stopover at Kranonos railway station where their Greek train crew refused to go on,

The main force of Kampfgruppe Balck journeyed south from Katerini to Platamon on April 15. In the column was this Panzerbefehlswagen III Ausf. E, a command tank (note the special antennae frame on the rear deck). On paper, Panzer-Regiment 3 had six such vehicles: two in the Regiments-Stab (Regimental HQ) and two in the Stabs-Kompanie of each of the two Abteilungen (tank battalions). Thus, Kampfgruppe Balck would have had four: the two of the Regiments-Stab and the two of the I. Abteilung. However, there may have been less on strength at this time. The small 'R' seen on the hull side of this tank denotes it was a Regimental vehicle. (USNA StM 143-16)

fearing the line ahead was damaged. The situation was solved by Major Henry Guinn from the 2/5th Australian Battalion who set off for Larissa with a New Zealand engineer, the latter having just arrived on a jigger (motorised railway inspection trolley).

Meanwhile at dawn on April 15 the 21st NZ Battalion on Platamon ridge was subjected to an hour-long heavy bombardment from the German artillery, few casualties being suffered because their weapon pits had been dug out of solid marble. Some fire was directed against Williams' troop of 25-pounders but the German spotter planes had dropped their flares 200 metres short of the guns and no damage was done. This was followed shortly after by an attack by three companies from Kradschützen-Bataillon 2. These were soon detected working their way through the scrub in front of A Company and when they emerged from it they came under intense small-arms fire from both A and B Companies resulting in heavy casualties among them. One group stumbled into the post led by 2nd Lieutenant Bill Southworth from No. 7 Platoon but these he beat back with the improvised grenades the engineers had made for him, one of them killing a German company commander.

This SdKfz 10 half-track apparently needed to be towed out of a stream by a PzKpfw III. Though not much is known about the tactical marking system employed by Panzer-Regiment 3 at this time, it would appear that playing card symbols on the turret were used to distinguish platoons in the 1. Kompanie, clover denoting 1. Zug (Leutnant Alfred Dörschmann), spade 2. Zug (Leutnant Brunnenbusch) and diamond 3. Zug (Leutnant Werner Parwoll). Platoon commanders would have a circle around the card symbol. Thus, the tank seen here was that of Leutnant Parwoll. (USNA StM 143-26)

At one point the route passed under a railway culvert but by way of the stream it crossed, necessitating some of the vehicles to wade through the rivulet to get past. The tactical symbol on the mudguard of this SdKfz 10 half-track identifies it as belonging to a towed anti-tank gun company, in this case the 2. Kompanie of Panzerjäger-Abteilung 38. Note the steel railway sleepers by the side of the brook. (USNA StM 143-28)

Another SdKfz 10 of Panzerjäger-Abteilung 38 towing a 5cm PaK 38 anti-tank gun. (USNA StM 143-30)

Another German column, advancing towards Palaios Panteleimonas on the right flank, ran into C Company and was soon pinned down by intense fire and withdrew, though in the process the Germans established the limits of the New Zealand position. After this, German artillery blasted the ridge with fire for the rest of the afternoon.

Around 4 p.m. the main force of Kampfgruppe Balck – the I. Abteilung of Panzer-Regiment 3 and infantry from the I. Bataillon of Schützen-Regiment 304 – reached Platamon ridge, Macky's radio message to Freyberg at 4.35

As it got closer to Platamon, the Kampfgruppe column broke cover from the woods and moved into more-open ground. Here two PzKpfw IIIs of the I. Abteilung of Panzer-Regiment 3 venture out in the open. As can be seen from the '122' on the turret, they belong to the 2. Zug of the 1. Kompanie, and the circled spade symbol on the turret of the lead tank identifies it as the mount of the Zug commander, Leutnant Brunnenbusch. (USNA StM 143-25)

Artillery was set up at the edge of the woods to fire on the New Zealand positions on Platamon ridge, among them this 15cm sIG33 self-propelled gun. It belonged to schwere Infanterie-Geschütz-Kompanie (mot. S) 703, which fielded six of these guns. (This particular type of sIG 33 SP gun – mounted on the chassis of a PzKpfw I – was quite rare, a total of just 38 being built in 1939-40. Six each were distributed to the 1., 2., 5., 7., 9. and 10. Panzer-Divisionen in March 1940, with two kept in reserve.) The company was commanded by Hauptmann Peter-Henrik Krambeck. (USNA StM 143-15)

Also set up to engage the New Zealand positions was this 7.5cm leichtes Infanteriegeschütz 18. (USNA StM 143-050)

Fire from New Zealand artillery lands on German troops operating below Platamon Castle. (USNA StM 143-32)

p.m. noting that a large convoy of troops had arrived. This he followed up at 4.56 p.m. to report that 25 tanks had assembled below the castle ridge, followed by one at 5.16 p.m. stating that the tank concentration had reached at least 150.

Balck finally made his move at 6 p.m., launching an attack between A and B Companies. Five PzKpfw IIs – the leichte Panzerzug (light tank platoon) of the 2. Kompanie of the I. Abteilung under Leutnant Giesse – tried to force their way up the high ground, the New Zealanders responding with Boyes anti-tank rifle fire, only to see them raise sparks off the armour. One tank got in behind No. 8 Platoon but could not complete the climb and was forced to pull back. Two halted underneath No. 9 Platoon and another got past No. 10 Platoon but had to give up because of the steepness of the terrain. In due course, all five PzKpfw IIs shed their tracks and had to be abandoned in no man's land between the German and New Zealand positions. Another seven panzers then tried to drive up a ravine between Nos. 11 and 12 Platoons from B Company but were turned back by mortar and artillery fire.

Further back, at 6.45 p.m., Veiel ordered the 8. Kompanie of Regiment z.b.V. 800 'Brandenburg' (a commando-type unit attached to the division by corps) to pass around Platamon by sea and drive up the Pineios river in assault boats with the aim of capturing the bridge at Tempi but this had to be called off because of rough seas. Later on that night, two companies from Kradschützen-Bataillon 2 worked their way up towards C Company at Palaios Panteleimonas, while the third climbed higher to outflank the defences. The attack eventually went in before the third company was ready and though they entered Palaios Panteleimonas Lieutenant Michael O'Neill led No. 13

A pair of PzKpfw IVs from the 3. Kompanie of Panzer-Regiment 3 on the beach north of the castle. The entrance of the railway tunnel can just be made out in the distance on the left. The composition of the I. Abteilung of Panzer-Regiment 3 at this time was as follows: the Abteilungs-Stab (Battalion Headquarters) had five PzKpfw IIs, the 1. and 2. Kompanie were each equipped with five PzKpfw IIs and 12 PzKpfw IIIs, and the 3. Kompanie had five PzKpfw IIs and ten PzKpfw IVs, giving a total strength of 54 light and medium panzers. (George Handrinos)

Today Akti Platamona beach is more a playground for people rather than tanks, with cafés along the foreshore. (Google)

Platoon in a counter-attack, driving the Germans out of the village and off another spur. Following that, the Germans retired to the base of the ridge for the night, launching a small incursion around midnight that was beaten back. For the rest of the night both sides came under intermittent shell-fire.

There were signs of more problems for Veiel. The division received a report from a staff officer for military traffic that the road between Yidha and Katerini was now so bad that their transport vehicles, predominantly

The commander of a PzKpfw IV examining Platamon Castle and the area below with his binoculars. The number 314 (just visible with a magnifying glass on the side of the hull to the left of the Balkenkreuz) indicates that it belongs to the 1. Zug of the 3. Kompanie. During the attack of April 16, Oberleutnant Wolf-Heinrich von Trotha's 3. Kompanie was initially in reserve, being only called forward later. (Jeffrey Plowman Collection)

The position of the castle establishes the location as being on the beach north of the railway tunnel near where today stands the Nostalgia Taverna, one of many beach bars along Akti Platamona. (Google)

Opel Blitz trucks, were scratching their floor pans and underbellies on the road surface, forcing traffic to a crawl of 5-10 kilometres per hour.

Elsewhere things had not gone well for the Germans either. The attempt by the 9. Panzer-Division to secure the Servia Pass had been an abject failure and Generalleutnant von Hubkicki was forced to pull the remnants of the attackers back across the Aliákmon river. Though he was keen to try again, Stumme, the XXXX. Armee-Korps commander, now decided to bypass this position, instead ordering the newly-arrived 5. Panzer-Division (General der Panzertruppen Gustav Fehn) toward Grevena and Kalabaka.

Unfortunately for the Allies, the response by W Force to all this was somewhat muddled. The British 1st Armoured Brigade continued their withdrawal but by the time they reached Grevena mechanical failures had reduced the 3rd Royal Tanks to six functional A10 Cruisers. At the Servia Pass the withdrawal of the 19th Australian Brigade and the 26th NZ Battalion began with the former heading south through Larissa, while the latter rejoined the 6th NZ Brigade around Elasson. Into this confused situation came the 2/7th Australian Battalion, reaching Larissa railway station around midnight only to find just the Greek stationmaster there, certainly no one from Anzac Corps HQ, nor any transport to take them to their ordered destination, Kalabaka, 80 kilometres away to the west. Eventually contact was made with Brigadier Ernest Lee of W Force Headquarters who told them: 'The show is over and a defensive line is to be occupied at Domokos'. Unfortunately, by this stage some fleeing Greek soldiers had taken over the battalion's train and were on their way back to Athens. On being told this Lee responded: 'The problem is yours', and promptly left. Undeterred, and with Larissa by then under aerial bombardment, the Australians fired up another engine but left the firebox door open. Then, while the Germans bombed that part of the station yards, they set about assembling another train around a second engine well removed from the first. It was finally ready that morning and on it the battalion set off for their new destination, Domokos.

To make matters worse, Anzac Corps HQ seemed unsure of how to deal with the situation at Platamon ridge. Around 11 p.m. on the night of April 15/16, realising how serious the situation was, Rowell approached Blamey with the suggestion that they send an officer to investigate. However, Blamey objected to Rowell's choice of Brigadier Cyril Clowes, the corps' CRAA (Commander Royal Australian Artillery), and proposed someone else but Rowell persisted and eventually got his way. The problem for Clowes, now, was that Anzac Corps Headquarters had no idea of what route he should take other than the fact that the position was difficult to access. In the end he set off at 1 a.m. on April 16 for Freyberg's division headquarters at Dholikhi, with orders to take any action he thought necessary. Rowell then contacted Macky at Platamon and told him to 'stick it out . . . a senior officer is on his way to assist and advise'.

Clowes' visit to the New Zealand Division Headquarters was not particularly fruitful. Talking to Freyberg and his Chief-of-Staff, Colonel Stewart, Clowes 'was unable to obtain any definite information as to the route, beyond the fact that access was difficult by road and that it was advisable to arrange for some means of rail transport – railway engine or jigger – from Larissa, railway being the only certain method'. Armed with this information, Clowes proceeded to Larissa reaching there around 6 a.m. but found the station area deserted, the town having suffered an early-morning bombing raid. Nor could he find anyone at 81 Base Sub-Area, so after two hours of fruitless searching he continued onto the Pineios gorge by road. Even then the road proved to be rough. Fortunately, on reaching the transport lines of the 21st NZ Battalion they lent him a 15-cwt truck.

In the meantime, from signals sent before dawn, the Corps GSO2 (Operations), Lieutenant-Colonel Cyril Elliott, woke Rowell to say that German tanks were breaking through on the right. With Blamey still asleep, Rowell immediately ordered Elliott to intercept the first troops of the 16th Australian Brigade and direct them towards the Pineios gorge. Informing Blamey of this on their way to breakfast, another argument ensued. Blamey had wanted to send the NZ Divisional Cavalry but Rowell won out in the end.

BREAKTHROUGH AT PLATAMON (April 16)

THE MORNING OF APRIL 16 found Freyberg's division under attack by the 2. Panzer-Division at two places, the Olympus Pass and Platamon ridge. While the Servia Pass had been held by the 4th NZ Brigade, with no sign of the 9. Panzer-Division following up, an Ultra intercept (OL 2075) received that morning indicated that the Germans [5. Panzer-Division] had crossed the

On April 16, Kampfgruppe Balck launched its main attack against the ridge, sending tanks and infantry towards the castle and the railway tunnel, with more infantry coming in on the right flank via Neos Panteleimonas. The attack succeeded but not without considerable losses. One PzKpfw IV of the 3. Kompanie ran onto a mine and caught fire. (USNA StM 144-09)

Its companion, a PzKpfw III, appears to have shed a track in the same depression. (USNA StM 144-08)

Aliákmon river the previous day to the south-west of Kozani (i.e. west of the Servia Pass) against limited opposition.

It was the situation at Platamon, however, that was to cause the most concern. During the night and early hours of the morning of April 16, troops from Kradschützen-Bataillon 2 had moved forward to below the ridge occupied by 21st NZ Battalion's C Company, while men from the I. Bataillon of Schützen-Regiment 304 had been working their way through the flank of the hills above C Company to get in behind them. Around dawn Kradschützen-Bataillon 2 and a company of Schützen-Regiment 304 attacked C Company around Palaios Panteleimonas, the attack falling first on 2nd Lieutenant Charles Mason's No. 15 Platoon. This was scattered by fire from No. 7 Section and the battalion mortars but the Germans soon regrouped and in a short time overran the section, followed shortly after by the rest of No. 15 Platoon. Captain Tongue, the company commander, sent out a patrol from No. 13 Platoon under Lieutenant O'Neil to help No. 15 Platoon but they returned after finding the latter's positions empty. Fortunately, some survivors from

The Panzer IV eventually blew up in a spectacular fashion, the explosion lifting the entire superstructure and turret off the tank and dropping it alongside. (Stefano di Giusto)

No. 15 Platoon managed to make their way back to Company Headquarters, which by now was virtually surrounded. These men and Company HQ eventually escaped the trap and started to withdraw down the other side of the ridge, this under covering fire from No. 13 Platoon.

Oberst Balck renewed his assault at 9 a.m., after a long preliminary bombardment by two batteries of Artillerie-Regiment 74. This time, he committed the 2. Kompanie (Leutnant Rudolf Wassmann) of Schützen-Regiment 304 against the castle, tank support being given by the 1. Kompanie (Hauptmann Albrecht von Boxberg) of the I. Abteilung of Panzer-Regiment 3. To divert attention from the main attack, the Abteilung's 2. Kompanie (Oberleutnant Harald von Nostitz-Wallwitz), accompanied by infantry, worked their way towards the railway tunnel but found this route blocked by the demolitions there.

In the centre the tanks of the 1. Kompanie forced their way over rocks, and through scrub and a mass of wire obstacles along a narrow mule path towards Neos Panteleimonas, while their accompanying infantry attempted to infiltrate between A Company on Platamon hill and B Company on Point 266. All through this hardly a trace of the New Zealanders was seen, apart from the occasional infantryman breaking cover and running back. As the panzers made their way up via a narrow mule track, several shed tracks or split assemblies until the leading troop ran onto a minefield, one PzKpfw

Note the engineer checking the site for mines with an Aachen Type 40 mine detector. (Stefano di Giusto)

III becoming a casualty and being abandoned by its crew. With this way blocked, some tanks attempted to find another route but two became mired in a swamp. Nevertheless, this move threatened to cut off No. 12 Platoon of B Company, so the company commander, Major Le Lievre, ordered its withdrawal to No. 11 Platoon's position. When this attack failed, the 3. Kompanie of Panzer-Regiment 3 was sent up the same gully towards Neos Panteleimonas, two PzKpfw IVs running onto mines, one catching fire and blowing up. This move unsettled Lieutenant-Colonel Macky, particularly with the 25-pounders now short of ammunition.

In fact, the situation by now was quite critical as Macky's communication with Freyberg's Advanced Headquarters proved. Among the first of these, received at 9 a.m., was one stating that 21st Battalion's ammunition position was serious, the second 20 minutes later reported that their left-flank company was in a precarious position and almost surrounded by an enemy battalion. To make matters worse, these messages arrived by a convoluted process that involved them being routed through Advanced Headquarters

Nearby, a Panzer III lies abandoned, the loss of the right track suggesting that it ran onto a mine too. This vehicle, as the number 101 shows, was in fact the mount of the commander of the 1. Kompanie, Hauptmann Albrecht von Boxberg. (Stefano di Giusto)

It was knocked out about 400 metres from the car park below Platamon Castle on the saddle between it and Point 266. Comparison taken by Nikos Valasiadis. (Nikos Valasiadis)

PK-Bildberichter Dick was on hand to capture the moment when another of the Panzer IVs ran onto a mine. The German caption to these photos, when published in the propaganda magazine *Signal*, read: 'A horrible detonation! Somebody shouts "Achtung, Minen!" but the result is not nearly so bad: in spite of the sizable mine crater, the tank is nearly undamaged. Only the right-hand track has run off its sprocket and one man, who has jumped out of the vehicle, is lightly wounded.' (ATL DA-11612)

to 5th NZ Brigade Headquarters with no instruction to copy them to Divisional Headquarters. Because of this, Advanced Headquarters paid no attention to the messages until they received a call about them from 5th Brigade Headquarters! Though this showed a serious lack of attentiveness by Advanced Headquarters, more vigilance by them would not have helped the 21st Battalion, their fate having been sealed by the intransigence of Anzac Corps HQ in providing support for Macky's men in the first place. Instead, all the New Zealanders at Advanced Headquarters could do was follow the denouement of the battalion as the final messages came through. The next one of these was received at 10.15 a.m. stating: 'Inf. attack left flank. Situation serious. Am standing by WT for your reply.' Almost immediately, another message was received: 'WT station 21 Bn closing down. Getting out.' It was at this point that Macky ordered a general withdrawal, after which he destroyed his wireless equipment. Before departing, Macky went forward to the artillery OP position and pointed out to Lieutenant Williams that, as there were no longer any infantry in front of him, he had better get out.

Macky's original intention had been to withdraw to a position a mile behind Platamon railway station but a quick survey by the Carrier Platoon revealed that this was not a viable option. Leaving the Carrier Platoon to

Another Bildberichter from Propaganda-Kompanie 690, Gerd Habedank, was with Kampfgruppe Balck on this day and he photographed some infantry near the same tank shortly after. (Stefano di Giusto)

As part of the April 16 attack, Balck sent a force of tanks up a narrow mule path towards the saddle between Platamon Castle and Panteleimonas. This photo, taken by a member of the division, shows a mixed column of PzKpfw IVs from the 3. Kompanie making their way up a gully. (Franz Steinzer)

The hill in the distance is Point 266 on which today Neos Panteleimonas is sprawling, indicating that tanks of the 3. Kompanie were operating quite close to the gulley where the 1. Kompanie was moving up. Today, a new thoroughfare, Frouriou Road, leads over the ridge and past the castle, which is away on the left. (Nikos Valasiadis)

cover their withdrawal, Macky then headed off in a carrier to the site of the Pineios river ferry below the village of Rapsani to reconnoitre an escape route for his battalion. Here the bulk of the battalion arrived platoon by platoon, dispersing under the mulberry and poplar trees on the river flats. It was around this time that Brigadier Clowes, the emissary from Anzac Corps HQ, finally arrived with orders that Macky was to offer any possible resistance at the ferry site and both the rail and road demolitions (in particular the latter) and must deny the western end of the gorge until April 19 'opposing the enemy advance with every means possible, even if it meant extinction'. Worse still, before Clowes left, the only measure of assurance he could offer Macky was that even if support was not on its way he would ensure that some was sent. Macky then made contact with Lieutenant Jones, the commander of the engineer section in the gorge, to complete work on the demolitions.

Shortly after Clowes' departure the battalion was joined by Williams' A Troop of the 5th NZ Field Regiment, which had travelled back by way of the railway. A number of culverts where the rails lacked supporting sleepers had proved to be an issue but these they crossed using some abandoned steel sleepers and wooden planks that they acquired along the way.

PzKpfw IV 321 (the mount of the platoon leader of the 2. Zug of the 3. Kompanie, Leutnant Hoffmann) was disabled after running onto mines below the castle, the detonation of which ripped off its sprocket along with its associated transmission cover. (Jeffrey Plowman Collection)

Nikos Valasiadis took the comparison from the same vehicle track beside the old Athens to Thessaloniki highway. Its position in relation to the castle indicates that it is some 300 metres from its junction with Frouriou Road. (Nikos Valasiadis)

B Company and the rest of C Company also arrived around that time and with that the business of ferrying the infantry and artillery over the river began, the first 25-pounder across being set up in an anti-tank position on the other side. The whole process was no sooner complete and the battalion safely across, when two shepherdesses arrived with their flocks of sheep and goats requesting a passage. These too were dutifully carried across the river, leaving the battalion alone at the ferry site. Macky, however, abandoned the idea of defending the eastern end of the gorge and so the battalion continued its retreat along the river road, the guns being towed back to Tempi by the battalion's lorries. Finally the battalion's Pioneer Platoon undid the wire rope from the pontoon ferry and threw it into the river. The ferry itself was sunk by Bren gun fire. Meanwhile, the carriers and other vehicles travelled back by way of the railway line.

Jones' engineer section then set about carrying out the demolitions in the gorge, though not without some difficulty. Undeterred by having used up all

A German soldier examines the track and sprocket of yet another PzKpfw IV that ran onto a mine during the attack. The soldier on the left is checking the terrain with an Aachen Type 40 mine detector. (USNA StB 135-02a)

A captured soldier being marched away under escort along the railway line from the castle. The official German caption described this this prisoner as 'the first captured New Zealander'. (USNA StM 144-10)

Shortly after, the same soldier was pictured on the deck of the Panzerbefehlswagen III Ausf. E command tank of Oberst Balck, the commander of Panzer-Regiment 3, seen standing up in the turret. (USNA StM 144-12)

Left: Besides Walter Dick and Gerd Habedank, there was yet a third Bildberichter covering the battle that day, Theodor Scheerer, also from Propaganda-Kompanie 690. He lost no time taking a close-up shot of the forlorn-looking prisoner. This image was clearly good propaganda stuff and it appeared on the front cover of the *Stuttgarter Illustrierte* of April 30, 1941 and also on the rear cover of the propaganda magazine *Signal* in June. The image was also 'wired' to New York from Berlin and from there to New Zealand on April 22. It was published in the *New Zealand Herald* on May 1, 1941, with the caption 'Somebody's son: a weary New Zealand soldier captured in Greece'. He was in fact 37-year-old Private Ray Irwin of the 21st NZ Battalion. Irwin had been buried alive when a mortar shell exploded nearby, killing some fellow soldiers. He was saved after some Germans spotted his hand poking out of the ground and dug him out. When the picture appeared in the *Herald*, his wife Pauline, who lived in Sandringham, Auckland, saw it and recognised him. The day Irwin was released from Stalag XVIII-A prisoner of war camp at Wolfsberg in Austria in May 1945, he was given the cover of the *Stuttgarter Illustrierte* by one of the guards and took it home as a souvenir. (BA Bild 101I-163-0315-03)

The distinctive hill seen behind Irwin is again Point 266, the position defended by B Company of the 21st Battalion. This comparison was taken at the point where Frouriou Road swings away from the railway line. Here a stream runs through a small gulley up to Point 266. A ridge separates this gulley from the one directly below Platamon Castle (the one up which Frouriou Road ascends to the saddle between the castle and Point 266). This suggests that this was the route along which Kampfgruppe Balck launched its main attack on the New Zealand position, the ridge between the two gullies sheltering the attacking troops from fire from Castle Hill until the last possible moment. As the comparison shows, the town of Neos Panteleimonas has today expanded onto the hill itself. (Nikos Valasiadis)

their explosives at Platamon, they found some in a railway hut across the river and, after the last carrier had dragged a boxcar from a siding into one of the tunnels they blew off its undercarriage. They then blew craters outside both entrances to the tunnel and demolished a nearby culvert. The resulting explosion of the latter blew the rails so high into the air that they came down on the other side of the gorge. In the meantime the sappers on the south side of the river completed the digging of two pits in the road with tools borrowed from a Greek road worker but could do no more as they had no explosives to put in them.

On hearing of the withdrawal of the 21st Battalion, the divisional CRE, Lieutenant-Colonel Clifton, ordered his other two sections to prepare the bridges over the Pineios at Larissa for demolition, sending some of his men under Major Charles Langdon. Here Langdon discovered Jones' section

As part of an attempt to divert attention from the main attack, tanks of the 2. Kompanie accompanied infantry from Schützen-Regiment 304 as they worked their way forward to the railway tunnel. Judging by the proximity of the sea, this PzKpfw III was very close to the tunnel entrance itself when it threw a track, suggesting that some of the panzers here had even tried to advance up the hill in support of their infantry. (Stefano di Giusto)

was out of explosives, so arranged for Sapper Les Congdon to bring some more from the RE dump, the return journey involving a hair-raising journey in a truck heavily laden with explosives, while Larissa was under a heavy bombardment. With these, the railway bridge at Tempi was blown up and the rest of the explosives used to blow craters in the road at the two pre-prepared places. Leaving No. 10 Platoon to guard the road demolition, the rest of the 21st Battalion headed back to the western end of the gorge, Macky setting up his headquarters in a house in Tempi.

Though Brigadier Clowes had not been aware of it at the time he was in contact with Macky at the Pineios gorge, the task of reinforcing the position was well underway. The first unit of the 16th Australian Brigade out of the Servia area was the 2/2nd Australian Battalion (Lieutenant-Colonel Henry Chilton). At this stage, extraction of the battalions was proving difficult, there being no radios available so orders had to be brought up by liaison officers. When the battalion reached the main road at Elasson around 10 a.m. its carrier platoon set off for Zarkos, to the west of Larissa, after receiving orders from 16th Brigade Headquarters that the battalion was to establish a blocking position there. Chilton also received the same orders after reporting to brigade headquarters but on returning to his battalion received new instructions from a liaison officer from the 6th Australian

The horse-shoe marking seen on both sides of the turret was the emblem of the 2. Kompanie. (Akira Takiguchi)

Now that the Germans had secured Platamon ridge, they started work on getting the railway tunnel underneath it open for their traffic. On April 14, immediately after the New Zealanders had chased off a German advance reconnaissance detail that had come to scout out the area, engineers of No. 1 Section of 19th (Army Troops) Company had set off their demolition charges in the tunnel, blowing the rails at both ends, blowing a hole in the roof and bringing down most of its lining. Two days later, with the area now in German hands, German engineers, from the 2. Kompanie of Panzer-Pionier-Bataillon 38 and the 3. Kompanie of Korps-Pionier-Bataillon 48, began repairing the tunnel.

Division that the battalion was to go to the Pineios gorge and that he was to go to Anzac Corps HQ to be briefed on the situation by Blamey's Chief-of-Staff, Brigadier Rowell. After this, Chilton set off for Tempi, linking up with his carrier platoon in the process, the rest of the battalion following some time afterwards. Chilton and the 2/2nd Battalion Carrier Platoon reached the Pineios position around dusk and made contact with Macky at Tempi, the rest of his battalion arriving that night and bivouacking south of Tempi.

Around midnight, Brigadier Graham Parkinson arrived with the 26th Battery of his own 4th NZ Field Regiment to join Lieutenant William's A Troop of the 5th NZ Field Regiment. As for the rest of the Anzac Corps, the 5th NZ Brigade, after successfully holding off Kampfgruppe Koelitz in the Olympus Pass, withdrew to the top of the pass in preparation for their withdrawal behind the 6th NZ Brigade at Elasson.

Fortunately for the Anzac Corps, Balck's force did not follow up that day,

With Platamon ridge captured, Balck's forces were able to assemble in the open, free from any fire from New Zealand artillery. The presence of the mounted soldier suggests that these men belong to Aufklärungs-Abteilung 112, the reconnaissance unit of the 6. Gebirgs-Division, which had a cavalry squadron. They were attached to Kampfgruppe Balck on April 16, the third day of the battle. (Jeffrey Plowman Collection)

their first act being to hoist a flag on the castle after which they became focused on clearing mines around the area of the saddle. Balck's men also discovered the food that had been left behind; for the motorcyclists of Kradschützen-Bataillon 2 it was particularly welcome as they had not eaten for 20 hours.

No such constraints existed for the 6. Gebirgs-Division. Around midday their Aufklärungs-Abteilung 112 (Major Friedrich-Karl Barth) and the 2. Kompanie of Gebirgsjäger-Regiment 143 (Oberst Georg Radziej) began a flanking move that would take them more directly over the mountains to the village of Gonnos in the Pineios valley where they would be in a position to attack Itia, across the river from Tempi. This route soon proved to be too much for the cavalry and bicycle squadrons of Aufklärungs-Abteilung 112, by then lagging badly behind, and they were ordered to make their way to the eastern end of the Pineios gorge and report to Oberstleutnant Decker, the commander of the I. Abteilung of Panzer-Regiment 3.

The photo was taken on the road that runs alongside the railway line at the point where it turns towards the coast and the northern entrance of the railway tunnel, the road essentially paralleling the original course of the railway line in 1941. (The current high-speed double-track line, which was opened in January 2004, continues straight on from here and passes under the ridge through a new and much-longer tunnel). (Jeffrey Plowman)

BUILD-UP AT THE PINEIOS GORGE (April 17)

THE SITUATION ON the morning of April 17, with Kampfgruppe Balck still at Platamon castle, was that the 6. Gebirgs-Division had reached Leptokaria, 40 kilometres south of Katerini, their advanced elements striking southwards over the mountains from Skotina (OL 2091). Further west, the 5. Panzer-Division, having reached Grevena the previous evening (OL 2098), had received orders to either swing back towards Elasson or continue on towards

April 17 saw the continuation of the withdrawal of the British 1st Armoured Brigade, accompanied by further losses of tanks by the 3rd Royal Tanks, all from mechanical failures of one sort or another. Among them was this A10 from B Squadron commanded by Lieutenant Robert Crisp. After he had lost his own C Squadron tank on April 14 (see pages 34-35), Crisp had taken over this one but it threw a track after crossing the bridge over what he claimed was the Venetikos river. Crisp and his crew were ordered to protect the bridge while it was being wired for demolition and started to build a wooden barrier in front of it but they were told to abandon this and the tank soon afterwards. With this, the last of B Squadron's 16 tanks had dropped out (Mark McKenzie)

Kalabaka/Trikkala if the road that way looked suitable, while the Schützen-Brigade 'Leibstandarte-SS Adolf Hitler' was to close up on Kastoria (OL 2093). Meanwhile in the centre, the 9. Panzer-Division was to prepare for another attack on Servia (OL 2094), the pass above it still under the control of the 4th NZ Brigade.

That morning at the Pineios gorge Lieutenant-Colonels Chilton and Macky and Brigadier Parkinson conducted a recce as far as the demolition on the gorge road, then in conference planned the deployment of their troops. Though maps stated that the Pineios river was eight feet (2.5 metres) deep, and therefore considered to be impassable to tanks, some consideration was still given to an attack coming through the gorge from this direction.

Defence of the gorge itself fell to the 21st Battalion and, with Chilton's agreement, Macky dispersed his battalion on the lower slopes of Mount Ossa, deploying D Company at Ambelakia above B Company at the gorge entrance. C Company was to occupy a position between B Company and Tempi on a spur that ran down towards the river, its No. 13 Platoon taking up positions on the forward slopes at the lower end of this spur. A Company

Though Crisp maintained in his war memoirs *The Gods Were Neutral* that this happened at the Venetikos river, and his description of the gorge and the road leading down to it fits that of the approach road to the bridge over that river at Eleftherochori, seven kilometres south-east of Grevena, it does not fit the photo he took of his disabled tank. What does match better is this bridge over the Aliákmon river on the road between Grevena and Poros, some 10 kilometres further to the east, this view taken looking east. (Google)

On the morning of April 17, a path now cleared through the minefield, Kampfgruppe Balck began crossing the saddle below Platamon Castle as a first step in heading south towards the Pineios gorge. These PzKpfw IIIs from the 1. Kompanie of Panzer-Regiment 3 and a half-track have lined up for the climb up the ridge. Note the white tape on the hillside, denoting the area not cleared of mines. (Stefano di Giusto)

was placed in reserve behind Tempi, while a platoon from Headquarters Company was to defend Tempi itself, with the rest of the company behind A Company. Before moving off to their defensive area, the men gathered what tools and implements they could from the villagers, having lost most of these at Platamon. Even with these, preparation of weapon pits was not without its difficulties. The ground occupied by O'Neil's No. 13 Platoon was rocky and provided no cover at all. Using a shared crowbar and working through the night they were only able to scratch out some shallow depressions and build up small parapets in front of them. Chilton also supplied Macky with a telephone line that gave the latter direct contact with his own headquarters.

Chilton then went back to his own 2/2nd Battalion and placed his C Company south-west of Tempi, A Company north of Evangelismos, D Company three kilometres along the riverbank opposite Gonnos and the rest of his battalion south of Evangelismos. With the arrival of their tools the Australians began digging their weapon pits. Around midday his commander, Brigadier Allen, drove in to take command of what was to become known as Allen Force. On his advice Chilton moved D Company to the other side of the valley, positioning it in the vicinity of the village of Parapotamos,

L Troop of the 33rd Battery, 7th NZ Anti-Tank Regiment reached 21st Battalion's position around 3 p.m. Three of their four 2-pounders were quickly sited in defilade positions between C Company's spur and Tempi:

The track down from the ridge was described by the Germans as narrow and better suited for their Mark II tanks, of which they now had 'hardly any left'. It appears to be quite narrow even for this 15cm sIG33 self-propelled gun from schwere Infanterie-Geschütz-Kompanie 703. The name *Edith* below the gun barrel indicates that it was No. 5 gun within the company. (We saw another one of the company's seven guns on page 49).

Assuming that the modern road down from Platamon Castle to the coast (Frouriou Road) follows the wartime track, then the photo was most probably taken here, just below the saddle of the ridge. Unfortunately, growth of vegetation has now totally obscured the castle. (Google)

Looking back northwards down the railway line today. The track has been upgraded to a metalled road and is now Frouriou Road. Another major change is the Hotel Kymata on the beach. (Jeffrey Plowman)

Having finally reached the coast at the bottom of the track, the panzers, with the 1. Kompanie in the lead, transferred to the railway line. (BA Bild 101I-162-0293-13A)

Sergeant Archie Quinn's gun L3 behind a bluff near Tempi where the serpentine ran down from Ambelakia; Sergeant Daniel Cavanagh's L4 in an enfilading position behind No. 13 Platoon's spur; and L1 in between. The fourth gun, L2, was set up commanding the railway bridge and the southern exit of Tempi, in C Company, 2/2nd Battalion's area. Some Australian anti-tank guns arrived later that morning and were dispersed around the positions of the 2/2nd Battalion. The 25-pounders of the 4th and 5th NZ Field Regiments were set up south of Evangelismos. That evening, however, at the request of the Australians, Lieutenant John Franklin's gun from A Troop, 5th Field Regiment, and Sergeant Jeffrey Gunn's gun from F Troop, 4th Field Regiment, were moved into anti-tank positions behind Evangelismos to guard the road from Tempi.

Just a short distance further down the line the column encountered the first of a number of culverts. Most were quite basic, the track simply spanning the gap between the abutments with no sleepers under the rails, but this one was more substantial. Yet the crew of the PzKpfw III appear to be taking great care to cross it, positioning the left track on a concrete strip on one side and the other over one of the rails. (BA Bild 101I-162-0293-20A)

The culvert has changed very little, even the railings still being in place. (Jeffrey Plowman)

After arriving around midday, Captain James Hay from the 2/1st Australian Field Company RAE was ordered to go forward to Makrikhorion railway station and contact Brigadier Allen to see what engineer assistance was required. Allen directed him to the 2/2nd Battalion's headquarters at Evangelismos where Chilton ordered him to set two demolition charges six feet across a road where the river road passed the base of the spur occupied by C Company, 21st Battalion. When this was complete, Lance-Corporal Reginald Werry and Sapper Gilbert Brady from the company were left behind with instructions to blow the charges at 8.15 p.m.

Also reaching the valley around noon was the second unit from the 16th Australian Brigade to arrive from the Servia area, Lieutenant-Colonel David Lamb's 2/3rd Battalion. The original intention had been to withdraw the 2/1st Battalion (Lieutenant-Colonel Ian Campbell) from its positions above Servia but the liaison officer, after setting out in the dark, failed to find any of Campbell's men, stumbling into the 2/3rd Battalion's position instead. Not long after that, Campbell arrived and it was agreed that the 2/3rd Battalion should go instead, as it would take him another 12 hours to reach his own unit. However, there appeared to be a mix-up in the orders and instead of joining Allen Force, the battalion Headquarters Company, less the Carrier Platoon, made their way to a point on the road between Larissa and Trikkala, near Zarkos. Fortunately, their mistake was realised and orders reached them to proceed to a new position just south of a wetland to the east of Larissa. In the meantime, Lamb proceeded with the Battalion Police to Tyrnavos, where alternative possible routes from the Servia area met up, there to intercept the companies as they came in and re-direct them to the new position. This would have succeeded completely had it not been for the fact that the transport available to uplift the entire battalion was insufficient, three platoons at Servia needing to be picked up later, specifically Lieutenant Gidley King's platoon from C Company and Lieutenants Ronald Gordon's and Geoffrey Cahill's platoons from D Company. This transport eventually reached them later on the night of April 17/18, dropping King's and Gordon's platoons off at the original rendezvous near Zarkos around dawn the following morning. On finding the site deserted they assumed that the battalion had departed southward for the Brallos position (near Thermopylae) and set off in that direction. Cahill's platoon arrived at the same spot two hours later and, on making the same assumption, also headed off for the Brallos Pass. By this time, though, D Company's commander (Captain Robert McDonald), concerned about his missing platoons, sent the Battalion Police out to search for them. They managed to overtake Cahill's platoon a few kilometres south of Larissa and turn them around but, with the other two platoons some two hours ahead, the police gave up the search and returned to the battalion.

The last unit of the 16th Australian Brigade to be withdrawn from the Servia Pass, Campbell's 2/1st Battalion, also found itself being diverted westwards after reaching Larissa to a point five kilometres short of Trikkala, being bombed and strafed all the way. Once there, they managed to contact 6th Australian Division HQ who informed them that they had been ordered back to Larissa to defend the aerodrome from a possible attack by airborne or parachute troops, a location they reached around dusk on April 17. They were joined later by the 2/2nd Field Regiment and six 2-pounder anti-tank guns from the 2/1st Australian Anti-Tank Regiment. In addition to this, D

The second PzKpfw III in the column has also moved onto the culvert using the same method of crossing it. Some of the other tank commanders have chosen to veer off the railway embankment and ford the stream instead. The lead panzer on the railway carries a circled insignia on the side of its turret identifying it as a Zug (platoon) commander in the 1. Kompanie. Note the cavalrymen leading their horses past the armour – they belong to the Reiter-Schwadron (cavalry squadron) of Aufklärungs-Abteilung 112. (BA Bild 101I-162-0293-22A)

The construction of Frouriou Road cut away the embankment overlooking the railway line. Jeff took this comparison from across the road to get a clearer view of the bay. (Jeffrey Plowman)

A few hundred metres further on, a SdKfz 251 half-track (carrying infantrymen of the 2. Kompanie of Schützen-Regiment 304) and a staff car pass a seaside villa built on a small promontory. (George Handrinos)

Constructed in the 1930s, the villa was for a long time the home of the famous Greek poet, historian, writer and journalist Kostis Moskof (1939-1998), who created most of his work here; hence it is today known as the Villa Moskof. The building is now operated as a luxury rental apartment. (John Irwin)

Another view of the column at the villa, this time looking back northwards. The tactical marking on the mudguard of the SdKfz 10 half-track (visible on an enlargement) shows it to be from a towed anti-tank gun company, in this case the 2. Kompanie of Panzerjäger-Abteilung 38. (USNA StM 144-20)

A little further on, another PzKpfw III Ausf. F rumbles along the railway. (USNA StM 144-18)

Trees today largely hide the house and undergrowth encroaches on the railway. Part of the stone wall beside the track is still there, though further back and overgrown. Behind the photographer lie the first houses of the town of Platamon. (Nikos Valasiadis)

A short distance on, Kampfgruppe Balck reached the road that ran along the northern bank of the Pineios river towards the gorge. These PzKpfw IIs belong to the Regiments-Stab (Regimental Headquarters) of Panzer-Regiment 3. (USNA StB 144-32)

The R04 sign on the side of the hull denotes that this is the vehicle of the Regimental HQ's Nachrichten-Offizier (signal officer), a position that was then held by Oberleutnant Ernst-Georg von Malortie. (USNA StB 144-30)

Shortly afterwards, the tanks reached the point where the road linked up with the railway line leading into the gorge. The presence of two track lines suggests that this was in the vicinity of the Rapsani railway station. Note the R03 sign on the PzKpfw II, denoting the Regimental HQ's Ordonnanz-Offizier (aide de camp), a position then occupied by Leutnant Neumann. (USNA StB 144-33)

and E Troops of the 5th NZ Field Regiment set up a defensive position to the south of the airfield.

Later that afternoon in the Pineios area, with all its companies in place, Chilton's 2/2nd Battalion sent out two patrols. One from D Company crossed the Pineios river with the view to investigate reports of small parties of men and animals moving about on the high ground overlooking the village of Gonnos across the river. This patrol made contact with several German patrols and managed to bring back items of equipment and uniforms. Later Chilton ordered a second patrol into the gorge.

On the morning of April 17, while the New Zealanders and Australians prepared their defences in the Pineios gorge, Kampfgruppe Balck set off from Platamon. Leading the force were the tanks of von Boxberg's reinforced 1. Kompanie, along with Wassmann's 2. Kompanie of Schützen-Regiment 304 in their SdKfz 251 half-tracks. Accompanying them was the Radfahr-Schwadron (bicycle squadron), commanded by Oberleutnant Erwein Graf

At the time there existed no direct road link between Platamon and Larissa but the Germans nevertheless were expecting to find a bridge in the gorge, the I. Abteilung of Panzer-Regiment 3 reporting with surprise that 'the bridge at the station drawn in on the map is still under construction' and the 2. Panzer-Division war diary recording: 'Enemy retreats, infiltrated the Tempe Pass. Road bridge east entrance of pass not present.' (The Greeks had started to build a concrete bridge but it was far from complete in April 1941 – see page 129). There was also a ferry further down the gorge but this had been sunk by the New Zealanders after their retreat from Platamon. Faced with these unpleasant surprises, part of the column descended onto the riverbed, possibly to determine if it could be forded. (USNA StB 144-36)

zu Eltz, from Aufklärungs-Abteilung 112 of the 6. Gebirgs-Division. With debris still falling from the roof of the railway tunnel, making that route impassable, the armoured vehicles descended to the coastal railway via the saddle track but it was slow going. Several tanks threw tracks, while others suffered damage to their sprockets as well. To ease their passage, accompanying engineers blew up some of the projecting rocks. By 11 a.m. leading elements of the battlegroup had turned inland from the railway line and reached the hamlet of Egani mostly on foot, the coastal track being completely waterlogged by rain, but by 11.40 a.m. only half a tank company had successfully crossed over the pass at Platamon ridge. When they did turn off on the track to Egani, it turned out to be heavily mined and hard going for the column. The rain-soaked road was also badly in need of repair, material for that being obtained by demolishing a number of houses and fences along the way. At 3.20 p.m. the column reached the eastern entrance to the Pineios gorge where Balck set up his regimental command post. By

However, Kampfgruppe Balck had no time to wait for the repair of the ferry or construction of a pontoon bridge. Calling their engineers forward and leaving them to start work on the ferry and bridge, the entire battle group continued on into the gorge along the railway line on the north bank until they reached three tunnels in the vicinity of the Church of Agia Paraskevi. PK-Bildberichter Dick pictured a SdKfz 251/8 Krankenpanzerwagen (armoured ambulance vehicle) halted in front of the first tunnel.
(BA Bild 101I-162-0293-32A)

This particular tunnel was removed in the early 1970s when the bluff was totally cut away to allow the construction of a longer tunnel that bypassed a troublesome section of the line in the gorge. This is the portal to the new tunnel, which stands in the approximate position of the old one. (Jeffrey Plowman)

this stage, however, the tanks had only just reached Rapsani. With no bridges over the river and the ferry destroyed, Balck ordered the battlegroup into the gorge along the railway line.

Eventually the column reached the centre of the gorge near the chapel of Agia Paraskevi. It was here around 5 p.m. that No. 10 Platoon from the 21st Battalion sighted a tank 'lurching its way along the railway line on the opposite side of the tunnel'. They called for artillery fire but the forward

The second of the three tunnels had been effectively blocked by the New Zealand engineers, No. 1 Section of 19th (Army Troops) Company towing a boxcar into the tunnel and blowing off its wheels, blowing up the railway line on either side of the tunnel, and demolishing a culvert. Though the engineers considered they had only done a tolerable job, Balck's tanks could not get past, Panzer-Regiment 3 noting how 'thoroughly the English had carried out their demolitions'. Bildberichter Dick pictured bicycle troops from Aufklärungs-Abteilung 112, who had reached this point ahead of the armour, outside the blocked tunnel. (BA Bild 101I-162-0293-33A)

Forgotten and disused, with the railway tracks removed, the second tunnel is slowly disappearing under vegetation. (Jeffrey Plowman)

The bicycle squadron continued on towards the third tunnel but when they tried to advance beyond it they came under fire from No. 10 Platoon of the 21st NZ Battalion from across the river. Though the mountain troops responded with mortar and machine-gun fire, these were soon silenced by two infantrymen from No. 10 Platoon after they had climbed up a bluff that overlooked the railway. This forced the cycle squadron troops to seek shelter back inside the tunnel. This is its eastern entrance. (George Handrinos)

observation officer with them was unable to make contact with his guns, due to the winding nature of the gorge and the steepness of the hills around it. The Radfahr-Schwadron continued on towards the second tunnel only to discover the demolitions and with it the realisation that no further progress was possible on that side of the river. Pushing on beyond the third tunnel they came under fire from No. 10 Platoon. The cyclists opened fire on the New Zealanders with mortars and a machine gun but these were soon disposed of by Privates Claude McCabe and Cecil Clark after they had climbed up the cliff

The road through the gorge on the other, southern side of the river was blocked by two craters blown in the road by New Zealand engineers. These were to be defended by No. 10 Platoon. Based on map references, this is the approximate site of the craters as it looks today. It was here that the platoon came under fire from a German tank after it emerged from the first tunnel. The official New Zealand account records that the platoon was ordered to withdraw up the ridge, though this seems unlikely in view of the steepness of the bluffs here. The gulley on the left would also have been in the direct line of fire from the tank. So it is more probable that the platoon retreated further back along the road, a short distance sufficing to take them out of the panzer's sight. (Google)

The Greek-Orthodox church of Agia Paraskevi, located about midway in the gorge, is noted for its holy spring in a cave nearby, reputed to be especially curative for people with eye problems. Oberstleutnant Karl Decker, the commander of the I. Abteilung of Panzer-Regiment 3, established his command post in the church and, though it was shelled on the evening of April 17, it remained largely unscathed due to the overhanging rock face. (Jeffrey Plowman)

With their way ahead blocked, the whole column was brought to a halt along the railway line. The pause gave one of the tankers the time to snapshoot his PzKpfw III. Note the small station building on the left. (Franz Steinzer)

Jeff was exhilarated to find the station building still standing. Located just to the east of the long post-war tunnel, it can be reached by some steps either from within the church or further along the terrace. (Jeffrey Plowman)

behind them and poured fire onto the Germans. At this point the Radfahr-Schwadron was forced to pull back and hide in the third tunnel. The panzer from the 1. Kompanie then swung its turret around and opened up with its gun on the New Zealanders, forcing them to seek cover. Some of the fire from the cycle squadron and the tank also fell on the patrol from the 2/2nd Australian Battalion, seriously wounding two men and compelling them all to take cover. There they remained for another two hours until dusk, when they were at last able to withdraw. Their wounded were left behind for No. 10 Platoon to bring out later, which materialised when Macky recalled the platoon to Battalion Headquarters.

Though the New Zealanders had been driven off, Kampfgruppe Balck was still in a difficult position, its column stretching several kilometres back from the blocked tunnel. There were other issues as well. For the battlegroup there was the disturbing news that they would be entirely without the possibility of resupply. Despite the efforts of the division to repair the road from Katerini to Litochoro (midway between Katerini and Platamon), their

Further back along the railway line some of the PzKpfw IIIs were still having problems negotiating the track despite the fact that they could straddle the railway line, this one appearing to come very close to the bluff face, its left track constrained by the outside rail. The tanks are spread out at standard convoy distance, which was just as well because that night they would come under fire from the New Zealand artillery, the shelling repeating hourly almost till morning. (BA Bild 101I-162-0293-29A)

Looking east down the Pineios gorge today. The railway line is now disused, having become redundant by a new tunnel blasted through the mountains. (Jeffrey Plowman)

Its further progress blocked by the demolitions at the second tunnel, the entire column now stood spread along the railway line for several kilometres, the line of vehicles stretching back to outside the gorge. Among the latter were these SdKfz 251/4 half-tracks with their 10.5cm leFH 18 light field howitzers from Artillerie-Regiment 74. (USNA StB 135-07a)

wheeled vehicles could not get further south. Further back, the division's own supply route was not assured either, it being dependent on the repair of the road from Yidha to Katerini by the XVIII. Gebirgs-Korps.

At this point Oberstleutnant Decker, having been given command of all

The tactical symbol on the mudguard signifies the unit as towed artillery. Off to the side of the railway is a PzKpfw IV from the 3. Kompanie of Panzer-Regiment 3. (USNA StB 135-08a)

Balck had certainly come prepared for any eventuality, these troops unloading a Grosse Flosssack 34 (large rubber assault boat, capable of carrying seven fully-equipped men) that had been carried on the engine deck of a PzKpfw II from Panzer-Regiment 3 headquarters. The R01 sign on the rear would in fact indicate that it is the regimental commander's vehicle but we have seen (page 65) that Balck's mount was a Befehlspanzer III. (ATL DA-11614)

The tankers having discovered a route across the river, the next problem was for the panzers to negotiate the steep descent from the railway embankment to the river flats on which the Agia Paraskevi Church was located. The Panzerbefehlswagen III seen making the descent here is in fact the same one that was photographed two days earlier (see page 46). (USNA StB 155-11a)

Tanks were not very good at swimming rivers in the early days of the war but this is what the Germans did. Most accounts state that they found a ford in the middle of the gorge but this was not the case. Instead, Leutnanten Brunnenbusch and Schmitthemmer scouted out a route up the river, i.e. the tanks would enter the water at one point, drive a distance through the stream and then exit the river at a point further upstream. Apparently, some of the infantry on the north bank thought it safer and easier to cross the river by riding as tank passengers than by rowing across in a rubber boat, and Bildberichter Dick pictured a PzKpfw III entering the water with infantry riding on the deck. (BA Bild 101I-162-0294-03A)

With no obvious points for comparison, finding the exact entry point was difficult but it was likely to be somewhere in the vicinity of a tunnel that runs under the old gorge road to provide a safe passage to visitors to the Agia Paraskevi Church. (Google)

troops in the gorge, decided to find a crossing point for the tanks there. Leutnant Brunnenbusch and Leutnant Lutz Schmitthenner set out to reconnoitre a route across the river through a process of wading and swimming upstream. When they returned, a PzKpfw II set off along the same approximate route and successfully found landfall on the south bank. Five more panzers followed, though two were abandoned by their crews after slipping into deeper sections of the river. Once across, an attempt was made to bypass the craters blown in the road by going around them through the river but this only resulted in three more tanks ending up swamped in the riverbank. Nevertheless, by the end of the day Decker was able to report four tanks over the river fit for continuing the advance, all under protection of some troops from the cycle squadron. Unfortunately for them, their position

Having crossed almost to the other side of the river, the PzKpfw III with its load of infantry turns upstream. A dirt road ran through the gorge on the south side of the river. It can be seen up the embankment on the far bank. (BA Bild 101I-162-0294-06A)

Having dismounted on the south bank, Dick walked back upstream and pictured a PzKpfw III wallowing upstream, the water starting to pour over the glacis plate. Behind it, a PzKpfw II has just started its upward passage of the river, while another medium tank is poised to enter the water on the opposite bank. (BA Bild 101I-162-0294-10A)

Jeff found the comparison just beyond the suspension bridge, which today crosses the river just upstream from the Agia Paraskevi Church. Being late summer, the water level was a lot lower than when the Germans crossed. (Jeffrey Plowman)

Dick next captured the same PzKpfw III, now in slightly shallower water. The diamond marking on its turret identifies it as belonging to the 3. Zug of the 1. Kompanie. (BA Bild 101I-162-0294-11A)

Part of the terraced area that extends upriver from the church is just visible through the trees. It is tempting to think that the exposed shingle bed on which the angler is standing is the same one that the panzer was traversing in 1941. (Jeffrey Plowman)

was not without its disturbances. Though the artillery observers from D, E and F Troops of the 26th Battery had been unable to make contact with their guns, by either radio of telephone that afternoon when they spotted the German cycle troops venturing into the gorge, an hour and a half later Major Gordon Stewart managed to direct fire into the gorge, the result being that the troops there suffered three killed and 17 wounded.

That evening, not leaving anything to chance, Balck ordered Leutnant

A soldier from Panzer-Regiment 3 pictured an immobilised PzKpfw III, its crew sitting marooned on top. It too carries a diamond emblem, indicating the 3. Zug of the 1. Kompanie. (Franz Steinzer)

This photo, taken later, shows two of the swamped tanks, a PzKpfw II and PzKpfw III, abandoned in the river, the former with only its turret showing. The rear one has the diamond marking of the 3. Zug, so it could well be the same tank as in the previous photo. The leafless tree branches in the foreground also seem to match. (USNA StM 145-06)

German records state that three PzKpfw IIs and one PzKpfw III were lost in the river – two tanks on April 17 and two the next day – but in this photo alone there are one PzKpfw II and two PzKpfw IIIs (the rearmost one is the one carrying the diamond insignia of the 3. Zug), suggesting the numbers may be different. Note the railway embankment on the opposite side of the river. (Jeffrey Plowman Collection)

Trees now obscure the embankment but the portal of the second railway tunnel (difficult to see, hence arrowed) points to this being approximately the same location. (Jeffrey Plowman)

Wassmann's 2. Kompanie of Schützen-Regiment 304 along a cart track that led over the mountains toward Itia via the village of Rapsani, their object being to secure the western end of the gorge. Rapsani was reached around midnight but beyond it the going proved too much for their SdKfz 251 half-tracks and they were forced to abandon them and proceed on foot. Even then the difficult terrain and the intermittent shell-fire prevented their further advance that night.

Back at the base of the spur held by C Company of the 21st Battalion, the two engineers, Werry and Brady, in what was to be an anxious night, had to endure several more hours at the river-road demolition site after receiving

On April 17, only four tanks of the 1. Kompanie had reached the south bank but once the craters on the road there had been filled in on April 18 it became possible to bring the remainder of the 1. Kompanie across the river, followed by the 2. and 3. Kompanie in that order. This Panzer III Ausf. F belongs to the 2. Kompanie (note the horse-shoe marking). (USNA StB 135-32a)

The same tank climbing out of the river. Note the SdKfz 9 heavy half-track, no doubt on hand to tow out any tank that got swamped. It belonged to the Berge-Zug (recovery platoon) of the regimental Panzer-Werkstatt-Kompanie (tank maintenance company). (USNA StB 135-33a)

A PzKpfw IV of the 3. Kompanie wading through the water. As it approached the point of exiting the water (note the panzers already on the south bank on the left), it passed the tanks that had become swamped in the river. (ATL DA-11625)

Unwilling to wade the river, Jeff took this comparison from the suspension bridge. The view is westwards. (Jeffrey Plowman)

orders not to set off the charges until given notice. As the evening progressed, a number of friendly patrols passed by moving up and down the road towards the gorge. One patrol brought news that the Germans were crossing the river in boats several hundred metres downstream. Next, the Australian patrol returned, followed sometime later by two Bren carriers. A further delay was imposed around 9.30 p.m. when a major (probably Major Le Lievre of B Company) told them he was going forward in a truck to extract one of his platoons that had been cut off by the Germans. The truck finally returned at 11.15 p.m., the driver giving them the All-Clear. At that point they set off the two charges and departed.

In the meantime, over to the east and unbeknown to the Anzacs, the Germans continued with their

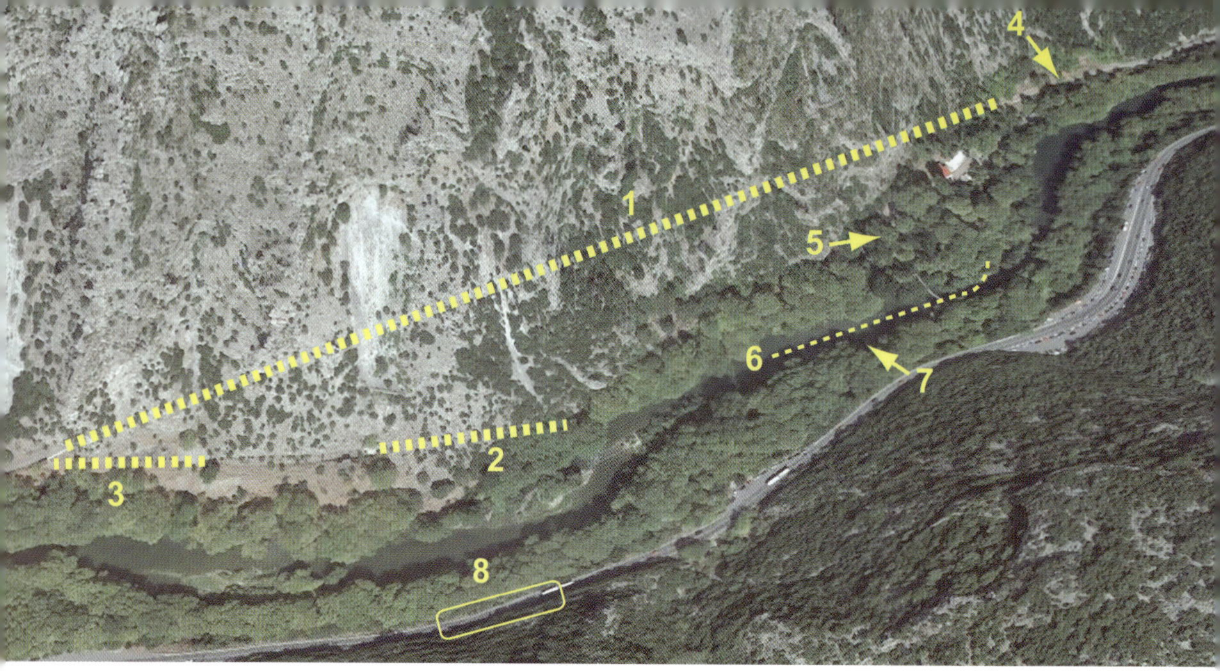

Aerial showing the main locations in the Pineios gorge today. [1] The new railway tunnel cut through in the 1970s. [2] The second tunnel, demolished by 19th Company, NZE. [3] The third tunnel. [4] Rapsani railway station. [5] Agia Paraskevi Church. [6] River route taken by the I. Abteilung of Panzer-Regiment 3. [7] Site of the three swamped tanks. [8] Approximate location of the demolitions on the south-bank road (map references place them directly opposite the tunnel demolitions). (Google Earth/Jeffrey Plowman)

outflanking movement, the 6. Gebirgs-Division working its way through the mountains on a parallel course to Kampfgruppe Balck. Having reached Skotina around 7 p.m. on April 16, they had continued on across difficult terrain towards Gonnos. At 6 a.m. the following morning, April 17, a number of Ju 52 aircraft dropped food supplies for them near Skotina. Around noon that same day, the advance guard of Oberst Radziej's Gebirgsjäger-Regiment 143 – the 2. Kompanie of the I. Bataillon (Major Heinz Wetzel) – entered Gonnos, the regiment's III. Bataillon (Major Josef Wieser) and II. Battalion (Major Helmuth Raithel) reaching the village during the night in that order. Both Kampfgruppe Balck and the 6. Gebirgs-Division had now reached positions from which they could launch attacks against Allen Force at the Pineios gorge.

Meanwhile the withdrawal of the Anzac Corps troops from the main defensive line continued. Taking advantage of thick mist over the Olympus Pass on the morning of April 17, Freyberg set in motion the withdrawal of the 5th NZ Brigade south to Thermopylae that day – a journey of some 180 kilometres – but not via Volos as originally intended. With parts of that road impassable due to heavy rain, the brigade joined the Australians on the road to Domokos and Lamia later that afternoon. That night, the extraction of the 4th NZ Brigade from the Servia Pass began, the entire brigade being pulled back to Thermopylae.

CRISIS AT THE PINEIOS GORGE (April 18)

WITH KAMPFGRUPPE BALCK and the 6. Gebirgs-Division poised to launch their attack against Allen Force at the Pineios gorge, an Ultra decrypt (OL 2108) received early on the 18th provided W Force with information on German intentions for the rest of their forces for that day. These were for the 5. Panzer-Division to continue on their line of advance past Kalabaka towards Trikkala and from there to Lamia, while the LSSAH was to be prepared to follow up after them. Having taken Servia, the 9. Panzer-Division was to push

Defence of the western end of the Pineios gorge was entrusted to Allen Force, the 21st NZ Battalion being placed at the head of the ravine around Tempi and Ambelakia, the 2/2nd Australian Battalion along the Pineios river from Parapotamos to Evangelismos and the 2/3rd Australian Battalion around Makrikhorion. (New Zealand Official History)

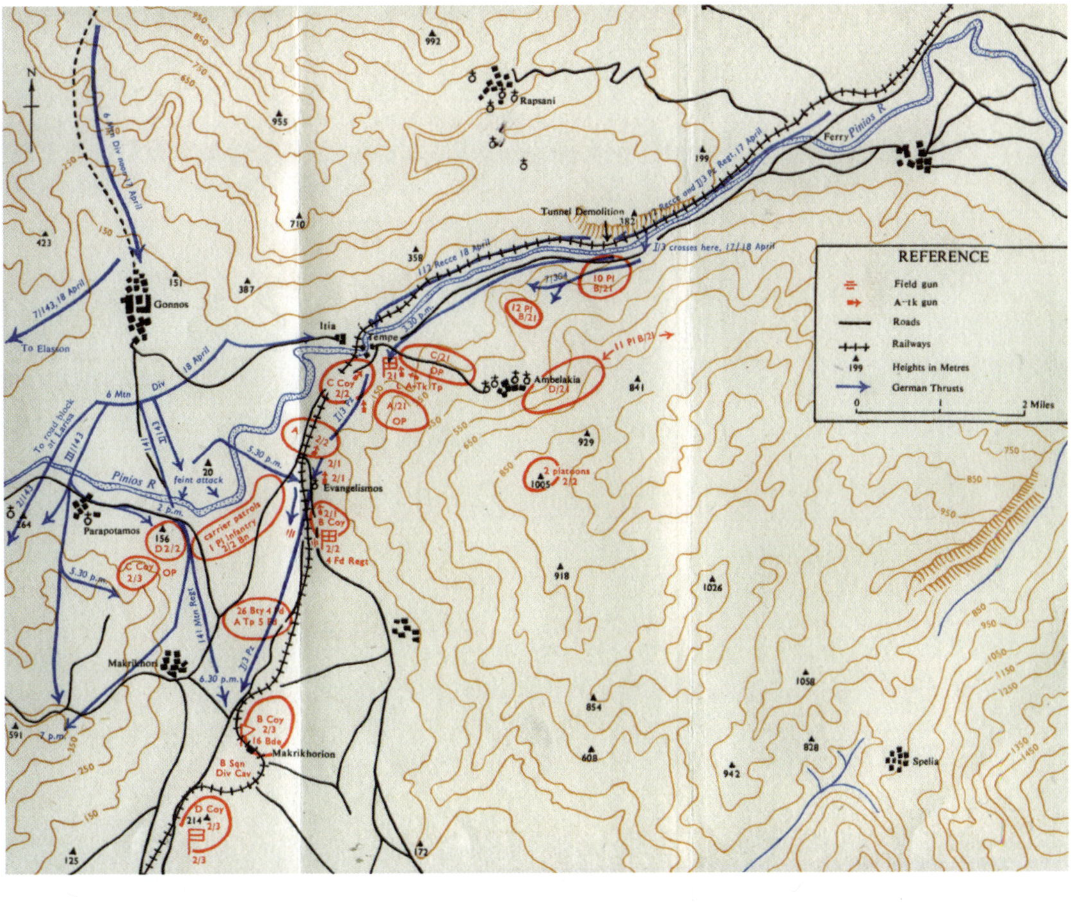

On the morning of April 18, Kampfgruppe Balck emerged out of the Pineios gorge, a platoon of infantry and five panzers attacking the 21st NZ Battalion in its new positions near Tempi taken up the day before. During this battle, Sergeant Daniel Cavanagh and the crew of a 2-pounder anti-tank gun – No. 4 gun of L Troop of the 7th NZ Anti-Tank Regiment – engaged the German tanks, destroying two of them (those commanded by Leutnant Brunnenbusch and Feldwebel Weber) and damaging the third. Cavanagh's abandoned gun was later photographed by a German soldier. (Franz Steinzer)

The picture was captioned in a 2. Panzer-Division history as being at Platamon Castle but the hills in the distance make it more likely that this is Cavanagh's gun near Tempi. It was positioned behind the spur on which No. 13 Platoon of the 21st NZ Battalion was sited. The lower part of this spur has since been cut away to allow the passage of the Athens to Thessaloniki highway but this spot along the old road to the gorge is the gun's probable location. (Google)

Barely visible on the upper superstructure of this PzKpfw III is the number 122, pointing to it being from the 2. Zug of the 1. Kompanie. (We saw this same tank on page 48). Though it appears undamaged, the spare wheel lying beside it and the absence of a hull machine gun suggest that it has been abandoned by its crew. The similarity of the ridgeline to the one behind Cavanagh's 2-pounder makes it likely that the tank is one of the three victims of this gun and, if not, then one of the three disabled by the other guns of L Troop shortly after. (Jeffrey Plowman Collection)

on towards Larissa but not to advance beyond the road fork at Elefterochori so as not to interfere with the advance of Kampfgruppe Koelitz from the 2. Panzer-Division.

On the morning of April 18, Lieutenant-Colonel Macky held his final conference with his company commanders, where he informed them that two Very lights would be the sign for them to withdraw to the flats behind Headquarters Company. Sometime later the appearance of Germans across the Pineios river around Gonnos and Itia was the cue for the start of an extended exchange of small-arms fire that soon escalated into an artillery duel.

That same morning, Lieutenant-Colonel Lamb's 2/3rd Australian Battalion received orders to move to a new position near the village of Makrikhori, three kilometres south of Evangelismos. From there A Company was sent to the villages of Bajli and Sykourion as a backstop against a potential paratrooper landing behind the battalion and B Company was moved to a position on the high ground north of Makrikhori to the left of the flank company of the 2/2nd Battalion. The rest of the battalion was kept in reserve north of the Makrikhorion railway station, all of the battalion having to manage without

On April 16, the day the New Zealanders retreated from Platamon ridge and out of the Pineios gorge, a decision was taken to blow up the railway bridge west of Tempi, so as to prevent the Germans from using it to cross the river. No. 1 Section of 19th (Army Troops) Company, NZE carried out the demolition, using explosives hastily brought up from Larissa. In the end, the blowing of the span proved futile as, the very next day, the German armour waded across the river deeper down in the gorge. The following morning, April 18, a platoon of mountain troops from Gebirgsjäger-Regiment 143 used the broken span to attempt to cross over and launch an attack on Tempi but they were driven off by heavy counter-fire. (ATL DA-11835)

The Tempi railway bridge has a decidedly chequered history. First built around 1905, and reinforced in the mid-1920s, it was first blown up by the New Zealand engineers. Repaired by the Germans, it was then blown up again by Greek partisans in 1943. The Germans repaired it a second time, replacing part of the span with a new section seen here, but then blew up the bridge themselves in October 1944 when they pulled out of Greece.

Resurrected again after the war, the bridge was bypassed during the construction of the new double-track railway line in 1996-2004. However, the now-disused span, and the track up to it from both sides of the river, still remain. Tree growth along the bank makes an exact comparison difficult. (Jeffrey Plowman)

anti-tank mines and barbed wire, these having been abandoned when they pulled out of the Verria Pass.

Around the same time, back at Larissa, the airfield was reconnoitred by Lieutenant-Colonel Campbell, the commander of the 2/1st Australian Battalion, with the view to defending it, though the plan was not put into effect.

German plans that morning called for the 6. Gebirgs-Division to launch attacks across the Pineios river with the intention of drawing attention away from the gorge. First, the I. Bataillon of Gebirgsjäger-Regiment 143 would make a feint attack on the left, towards the village of Tempi; next, the regiment's IIII. Bataillon would make the main attack on the right, towards Parapotamos. Simultaneously with the III. Bataillon's attack, the 2. Kompanie of the I. Bataillon, with an engineer platoon attached, was to cross the Pineios at a spot further to the west with the special task of thrusting over the western slopes of the Erimon mountains towards the Tempi–Larissa road and of blocking the road behind the enemy.

At 5 a.m. Aufklärungs-Abteilung 112 tried to break out of the third tunnel in the gorge, managing to reach a shrine further along on the railway embankment. Here they came under intense enfilading fire from mortar and artillery fire and were forced to go to ground.

At 6.15 a.m. a platoon from Major Wetzel 's I. Bataillon of Gebirgsjäger-Regiment 143, sent out to protect the left flank of the battalion's main

The broken railway bridge can be seen in this oblique aerial taken from a German reconnaissance aircraft. The view is westwards and the village of Gonnos, captured by Gebirgsjäger-Regiment 143 on the night of April 17/18, lies beyond the distant ridge. It was from there that they launched their assault crossings across the river on April 18. The hamlet of Tempi lies on this side of the river immediately below the aircraft. As can be seen, once out of the gorge (behind the photographer), the Pineios valley opens out into perfect tank terrain. At lower left is the road to Larissa, taken by Kampfgruppe Balck on April 19. (Jeffrey Plowman Collection)

crossing, came under heavy fire when they tried to clamber over the blown railway bridge at Itia and had to abandon the attempt.

At 8 a.m. Wetzel's battalion launched its main attempt to cross the river, striking out towards Tempi. In response, Lieutenant-Colonel Chilton, the 2/2nd Australian Battalion commander, sent forward his carrier platoon.

Without an aircraft to take an exact comparison, Stephen Hutcheon took this picture from the top of the sinusoidal road leading up to Ambelakia providing a remarkably close comparison to the aerial view. Both the old railway bridge and its modern double-track replacement are clearly visible. (Stephen Hutcheon)

They made their way forward to a small hill overlooking the river. After dispersing and concealing their carriers, their crews set up Bren guns on top and opened fire, focusing particularly on a group of Germans on a sand spit in the river and their supporting mortars. Mortar fire was also called down on the Germans and later on more fire came from the 26th Battery further back, the unit having registered their guns along the line of the river the previous day. Around 11 a.m. Chilton asked for support from Macky, who sent over his carrier platoon. This was probably the last time Chilton heard from Macky, communication between them ceasing sometime between 11 a.m. and noon. The combined fire was devastating to the Gebirgsjäger, killing most of those that had managed to cross the river and others still in it, and by 11.30 a.m. the German attack had been brought to a halt. More disquieting to the Anzacs, as the German survivors struggled to the shore, was how much shallower the river was, leaving some to question the reliance they had placed on the river as a natural tank trap.

Meanwhile, further to the west, Gebirgsjäger-Regiment 143 had launched its second and main attack across the river. At 8.30 a.m. Major Wieser's III. Bataillon moved down towards the river to the left of 2/2nd Battalion's D Company, fire from the Australian heavy machine guns and artillery increasing in response. After a patrol found a boat, the 12. Kompanie crossed over, forcing D Company to withdraw from around Parapotamos towards the high ground to the north-west of Makrikhori. The rest of the battalion assembled at the river shortly afterwards, crossing in assault boats under supporting fire from their divisional artillery.

Having been blocked in its first attempt by the Australians, Wetzel's I. Bataillon next tried to cross the river to the west of Gonnos but found the river there too deep and wide. Lacking material to make a bridge, and with most of his men unable to swim, Major Wetzel sought permission to use a ferry that Wieser's III. Bataillon had discovered east of Parapotamos. However, this was denied and instead he was ordered to move his battalion by all available means to Tempi. Wetzel refused to carry this out as it would have put them under flanking fire from the Australians.

While the two main attacks by Gebirgsjäger-Regiment 143 had been observed and met with fire by the Anzacs, one other crossing had escaped the latter's notice. At 9.30 a.m., tasked with setting up a blocking force where the road to Larissa crossed the railway line, the 2. Kompanie of the I. Bataillon, under Oberleutnant Karl-Peter Jacob, had swum across the river on the mountain division's extreme right flank, completely unnoticed by the Australians in the vicinity of Parapotamos. The non-swimmers and heavy weapons were brought across on rafts shortly afterwards. The presence of the Australians nearby, however, brought about a change of plans, Jacob leading the company on a wider outflanking movement.

Earlier that morning, two platoons of infantry – the 1. and 2. Züge from the newly-arrived 7. Kompanie (Oberleutnant Karl Mickley) of Schützen-Regiment 304 – crossed the river on kapok floats to join the by now five panzers of Panzer-Regiment 3 on the south side of the gorge. By midday, with both craters filled in, Mickley sent the 2. Zug back across the river with orders to collect their weapons and rejoin them as soon as they could. He then set off with the 1. Zug and the five tanks, the force bursting out of the gorge 15 minutes later. Two of the tanks and the infantry swung left towards B Company of the 21st NZ Battalion, opening fire and forcing them up the ridge. They then drove up to the foot of C Company's ridge and turned their fire onto Nos. 14 and 15 Platoons, driving them further up the spur of their ridge, towards the crest of the main ridge to Ambelakia. This also had the effect of lifting the fire off the cycle troops in the gorge, enabling them to start moving forward at 12.30 p.m. towards the Gebirgsjäger at Itia. At 1 p.m. Captain Trousdale, the commander of D Company, at Ambelakia observed two Very lights, the signal to withdraw along the plains below but, there being no way to do this now with the arrival of the tanks, he decided against following this order. By 2 p.m., having successfully eliminated both B and C Companies' positions, the two tanks set off in the direction of the Australian demolitions in the river road. Nevertheless, things were not going well, prompting Oberstleutnant Decker to contact Oberst Balck to report that the advance was taking a long time and request more support. Instead Balck responded: 'I don't want to hear from you until you have taken Tempi. I can't give you any more troops.'

While this had been going on, the other three tanks, among them the Panzerbefehlswagen III (command tank) of the battalion commander, Decker, and a PzKpfw III had closed to 100 metres of the spur on which No. 13 Platoon was based; too close in fact, their rounds either skimming over the top of the hill or embedding themselves harmlessly in the ground in front. At this point three men from the platoon ran off but the rest, unwilling to flee or surrender, held their ground as the three panzers continued to fire on them. One of the tanks eventually detached itself to join up with the two making for the road demolition site, the crew getting out of their tank to inspect the craters. The remaining two kept up the fire on No. 13 Platoon for an hour until some of the German infantry from the 1. Zug worked their way around from the lower slopes of Mount Ossa and rounded them up.

Then for the next half hour Sergeant Daniel Cavanagh and the crew of his 2-pounder from L Troop, 7th Anti-Tank Regiment, waited as each tank gingerly made its way across the demolition, the tank crews climbing out in turn to await the arrival of the others. When the last tank drove up, they climbed back in and, as they were settling into their stations, Cavanagh's gun opened up, setting the lead two – commanded by Leutnant Brunnenbusch and Feldwebel Weber – on fire. Of the two crews, only Weber got out unhurt, three men were killed, one was heavily burned and the five others, including Brunnenbusch, were wounded. Weber and the wounded escaped into the scrub. Cavanagh's gun then became involved in a firefight with the third panzer, loosing off a total of 28 rounds, until they were forced to make a hasty getaway by the arrival of some German infantry. At that point Decker's Panzerbefehlswagen III and the PzKpfw III drove over to help the wounded. Decker's driver, Feldwebel Grzeschick, and others managed to put out the fires with extinguishers before the panzers could blow up, and the regimental and battalion doctors, Stabsärzte Dr Marx and Dr Grametbauer, took care of the wounded. Hauptmann von Boxberg then called up his company's last four tanks and sent them off in the direction of Tempi, only to see three of them knocked out by the other 2-pounder guns from L Troop.

One of the obstacles faced by the remnants of Allen Force in their withdrawal from the Pineios gorge was the Nessonis swamp, about halfway between Makrikhori and Larissa, where the road narrowly passes between a marshy area to the west and a low line of hills to the east. On the night of April 18/19, several 25-pounders and their Guy Quad Ant artillery tractors from the 4th NZ Field Regiment got stuck in the ford through the swamp. (The '3' on the red and blue shield seen on the back of the vehicle was the unit serial number for the 4th NZ Field Regiment). (Robert Gregory Collection)

The picture was taken on the old Makrikhori to Larissa road near the village of Amphithea, the swamp having long since gone, drained to turn the area over to agriculture. (Google)

A column of vehicles led by a PzKpfw I en route to Larissa passing the same tractor and gun. The F5 marking on the side of the Quad identifies it as No. 5 Gun of F Troop of the 26th Battery of the 4th Field Regiment, one of the gun troops providing support for B Squadron of the NZ Divisional Cavalry when they were acting as rearguard during the withdrawal from Makrikhori. (NIOD 20914)

Sergeant Quinn's gun L3 near Tempi was knocked out by tank fire while L1 was destroyed by Oberleutnant Mickley, the 7. Kompanie commander, who attacked it with grenades. He was later awarded a Ritterkreuz for this action.

At 3 p.m. the Germans ramped up their attack on Tempi, Leutnant Pratsch's platoon from Aufklärungs-Abteilung 112 storming over the demolished bridge and swinging around to attack the village. After a short sharp fight No. 5 Platoon from Headquarters Company was overrun, the survivors falling back on A Company. Half an hour later, the one surviving panzer reached Tempi.

Concern over the situation developing around Tempi saw the arrival of Freyberg at Brigadier Allen's headquarters at 3 p.m., where he spoke to Lieutenant-Colonel Chilton over the field telephone. Freyberg then went forward to examine the situation in person and, on realising that the Germans could not be held until midnight, ordered contact to be broken at dusk. Having done all he could he returned to Larissa and, for a time, directed traffic at the main crossroads.

After Freyberg had departed, adjustments were made to the dispositions of Allen Force, some planned, some impromptu. At 4 p.m. Brigadier Parkinson ordered D Troop of the 26th Battery back to join B Squadron

German infantry using a track above the road to bypass the muddy site of the tractor and gun. The presence of the pack mules suggest that these are Gebirgsjäger troops. (Robert Gregory Collection)

The rock formations confirm that this is the same location. (Google)

(Major John Russell) of the NZ Divisional Cavalry astride the railway between Makrikhorion and Point 214, the latter having arrived there around midday.

While the attack on Tempi had been underway, better progress had been made by Major Wetzel's I. Bataillon of Gebirgsjäger-Regiment 143 at the Pineios river. Having seen both their crossing attempts that morning thwarted by the Anzacs and having been denied the use of III. Bataillon's ferry near Parapotamos, sometime around 1 p.m. they discovered that the river to the west of Evangelismos could be waded by way of a mud bank in the river. An hour later, taking advantage of this, they began pushing troops across it. Notwithstanding heavy defensive fire from around Evangelismos and from the south-east, this enabled the 1. Kompanie to quickly establish a bridgehead, where it was joined shortly afterwards by the 3. Kompanie, the speed of their advance catching the Australians by surprise. With supporting fire from their mortars the Gebirgsjäger continued to push troops over the river and by 3.30 p.m. the whole battalion was across, launching an attack towards Evangelismos shortly afterwards.

News of these events made its way further back to Larissa airfield and resulted in a succession of confusing orders. At 4 p.m. the guns from the 2/1st Australian Anti-Tank Regiment received orders to commence their withdrawal from the aerodrome at 5 p.m. This order was cancelled 15 minutes later after news had been received of German tanks breaking through at the Pineios gorge. An hour later this order was in turn cancelled on the basis that only five tanks had managed to penetrate the positions around the gorge, the anti-tank guns' move south eventually beginning at 7 p.m.

At 4.30 p.m. Balck reached Tempi and ordered Decker to continue the attack towards Larissa. With Hauptmann von Boxberg's 1. Kompanie no longer an effective fighting force and the 3. Kompanie still in the process of crossing the river, the task fell to the tanks of Oberleutnant von Nostitz-Wallwitz's 2. Kompanie. They were accompanied by the 1. Zug from Mickley's 7. Kompanie of Schützen-Regiment 304, neither the company's 2. Zug reaching them in time from Agia Paraskevi, nor Leutnant Wassmann's 2. Kompanie from Rapsani.

The attack fell upon A Company, 21st NZ Battalion, south of Tempi. Supported by a section of carriers the company held off the attacking German infantry for a time but the panzers eventually broke through, the leading one being forced off the road when Sergeant-Major Allan Lockett rammed it in his carrier. At that point the survivors of the company made for Mount Ossa to join the rest of the battalion in its retreat or headed south, some throwing away their weapons. Lieutenant William Southworth's No. 7 Platoon, however, kept theirs and joined forces with the main body of the 2/2nd Australian Battalion at Evangelismos.

Around 4.45 p.m. Lieutenant-Colonel Lamb ordered C Company of his 2/3rd Battalion, to withdraw and to coordinate this with D Company of the 2/2nd Battalion. Unfortunately, this caused D Company to begin to withdraw when it saw C Company pulling back, this occurring much earlier than

Chilton had intended, leaving him with the unfortunate impression that one of his companies had run away. Both companies were ordered by Lamb to take up positions at what was to become their first rearward position on the left flank of the 2/3rd Battalion main position on Point 214.

Von Nostitz-Wallwitz's tanks now turned their attention to the 2/2nd Battalion. Around 5 p.m. they linked up with the I. Bataillon (Major Förster) of Gebirgsjäger-Regiment 141 (Oberst Friedrich-Jobst Volckamer von Kirchensittenbach) that had just crossed over the river by means of the ferry at Parapotamos. The panzers fired on 2/2nd Battalion's C Company for half an hour before some of them, supported by infantry, pushed into the ground between the road and the river, while other German troops moved onto the high ground abandoned by the 21st NZ Battalion. The net result of this was to bring C Company under fire from three sides, eventually forcing it to withdraw to the high ground to the south-east when the panzers broke into their positions. At the same time several other panzers entered the

Another abandoned Guy Quad, this one from No. 4 Gun of F Troop, found by the Germans on their way to Larissa on April 19. (USNA StM 145-20)

positions of A Company, followed up by more shortly afterwards and these began milling around and firing madly. The company was also under fire from mortars across the river and as a result pulled out and made for the high ground to the south-east. At 5.55 p.m., with these positions abandoned, two tanks swung out from behind a spur in front of B Company and Battalion Headquarters south of Evangelismos. They were promptly engaged by a 2-pounder, Leutnant Langhammer's panzer being knocked out and set on fire, the other withdrawing after another round struck it.

The entire force of 15 to 18 tanks then deployed into the middle of the valley and turned in towards Evangelismos. This brought them into the line of fire of the two 25-pounders behind the 2/2nd Battalion. Sergeant John Franklin's gun from the 5th NZ Field Regiment hit and set two tanks on fire in quick succession, before they were forced to abandon the gun when another tank destroyed their ammunition limber. Sergeant Jeffrey Gunn's 25-pounder from the 4th NZ Field Regiment hit and set fire to two more tanks. Then a third came in and took up a hull down position before systematically searching for the camouflaged gun. At this point the crew manhandled it into a slight hollow 100 metres to their rear but they could not move all the ammunition, taking only ten rounds of armour-piercing with them. From here they became engaged in a duel with the tank (which they believed to be a PzKpfw IV) until their armour-piercing ammunition ran out. One of the gunners went back for more ammunition but while he was away a stray shell wounded the rest of the crew and they were forced to abandon their gun and retire too. However, all this was not enough to stop the attack on the rest of the 2/2nd Battalion and at 6.45 p.m., with the tanks closing in and with the Australian crew of their other 2-pounder having abandoned their gun without firing a shot, they too started up the slopes of Mount Ossa.

With this bulwark now gone, the seven remaining guns of E and F Troops of the 26th Battery, 4th Field Regiment were forced to fall back towards Makrikhori. Covered by E Troop, F Troop pulled back two kilometres, E Troop destroying two tanks and putting several more out of action. Next, two guns from E Troop withdrew a kilometre behind F Troop, leaving the other two guns to deal with the tanks, three more of the latter being knocked out, one of them being engaged at less than 100 metres and all but disintegrating when it blew up. Both guns then re-joined E Troop, while F Troop covered them. By now E Troop was out of ammunition so departed for Larissa but not before they passed through the 2/3rd Battalion's forward position on Point 214 where Lieutenant-Colonel Lamb tried to stop them at pistol point and turn them around. It was now F Troop's turn to withdraw, two of the guns joining D Troop. This left Russell's B Squadron of the NZ Divisional Cavalry out in front of the 2/3rd Battalion.

Around 7.30 p.m., after being bombed and strafed by the Luftwaffe, D Company of the 2/2nd Battalion and C Company of the 2/3rd Battalion found themselves up against 12 to 15 panzers approaching along the road, their turrets traversing and firing in all directions. Two 25-pounders near them turned on the tanks, destroying two of them before one of the guns was knocked out. The second gun, now out of ammunition, was limbered up and towed off. At this point the tanks broke into the position occupied by both companies. Corporal Bill Cameron of the 2/3rd Battalion climbed up onto one hoping to set it alight with a can of petrol but was thrown off when the tank began to swing about violently and then ran over him. He was quickly rescued and carried from the battlefield, fortunately the soft ground preventing him from suffering serious injuries.

At 9 p.m. under falling light the rest of the 2/3rd Battalion pulled back to the second rearward position, some 1,500 metres behind Point 214, covered by Russell's cavalry squadron. Under pressure as the panzers advanced through the trees, the squadron was steadily forced back, its armoured cars and carriers leapfrogging through each other. Several of the panzers received direct hits from the 25-pounders of D and F Troops and these panzers were temporarily forced to fall back. The carrier platoons also withdrew from the flanks, followed shortly after by D Company of the 2/2nd Battalion and Lamb's own C Company coming in from the left. Both companies were directed to the rear of the main body of the 2/3rd Battalion. At this point, more tanks emerged from the steadily increasing gloom in front of the second rearward position, the Australian infantry allowing one panzer to drive into their positions before they opened up and killed the commander, causing the tank to withdraw. Some of the panzers then gained the high ground overlooking the road in the hope of cutting off the retreating Anzacs but were unable to make further progress because of the marshy ground between them and the road.

Once more, Russell's squadron took over as rearguard while the 2/3rd Battalion withdrew to their waiting transport and the men began to climb on board. Here, in complete darkness, eight panzers came forward and became intermingled with the squadron vehicles, several of the latter receiving hits, though none serious. In the middle of this melee Russell's armoured car overturned and had to be abandoned, he and his crew being rescued by another car. In the confusion in the dark another cavalryman walked right up to a German tank, thinking it was theirs, before realising his mistake. This news was of sufficient concern for Brigadier Allen to consider forming another line behind the Nessonis swamp but half an hour after midnight (April 18/19) he received news that the rearguard had pulled back and the enemy had not followed them up.

In fact the German armour had withdrawn and formed a laager around their regimental command tank, their accompanying infantry from Mickley's 7. Kompanie providing protection from the south and west. With the Nessonis swamp ahead of them and their attack now spent, there was also the fear that they had been shooting at each other as well as the enemy, in fact a patrol from the I. Bataillon of Gebirgsjäger-Regiment 141 had been forced to the ground after they got mixed up with the tanks. Not only that but the tanks were by now so low on ammunition that they been forced to

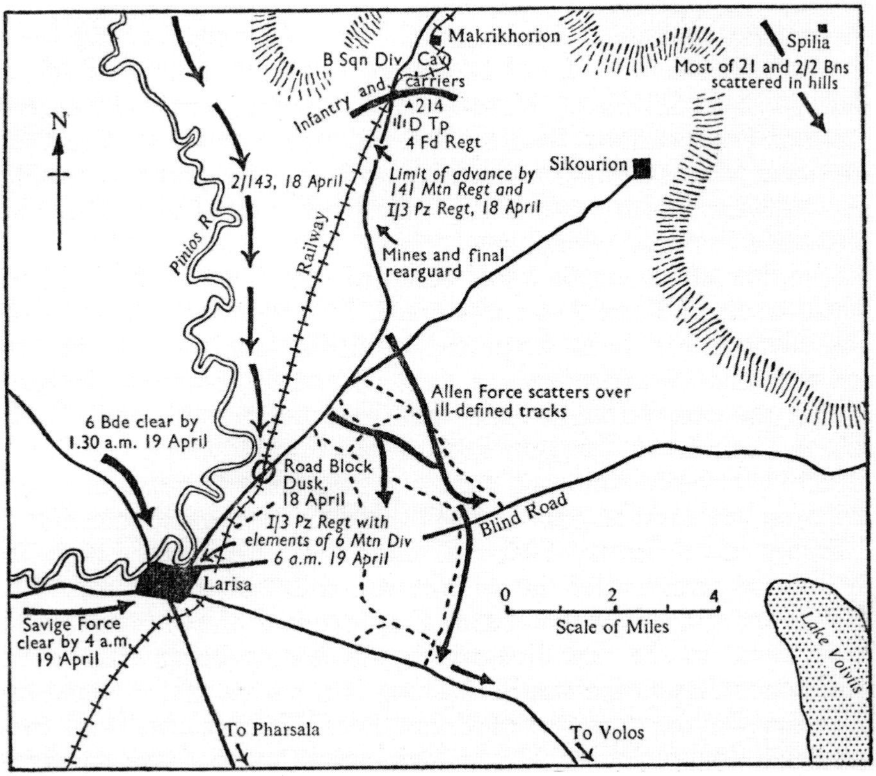

During the final stages of the battle, the 2. Kompanie of Gebirgsjäger-Regiment 143 established a roadblock where the railway line crossed the main road to Larissa. Thus, when the 2/3rd Australian Battalion fell back from Makrikhori, they ran into this blocking group, some 50 men, including 20 seriously wounded, being taken prisoner before the rest of the force escaped southwards over ill-defined tracks. (New Zealand Official History)

scrounge for it from the knocked-out tanks. They were also almost out of petrol.

This proved to be fortuitous for Allen Force. Ahead lay the Nessonis swamp, at one point only negotiable by a narrow ford. After a few trucks and carriers had passed through it a gun tractor got stuck in it. Though this obstruction was cleared quickly a logjam developed involving 20 Army Service Corps trucks that Brigadier Parkinson had brought forward to evacuate stragglers from the 21st NZ Battalion. Approximately 150 men from the battalion had come in around 7 p.m. and had only just been loaded onto the trucks when another 50 men appeared and were taken on board. The empty trucks, in trying to escape, ended up blocking the entrance to the ford and this took some time to clear. Several of the tractors and guns, in succession, also plunged into the side of the ford and their extrication imposed a further delay. Thus, it was not until 12.30 a.m. on the morning of April 19 that the ford was finally clear and the column commenced moving forward.

The elation in getting moving again was to be short lived. Closing in on Larissa the leading vehicles suddenly came under fire from Jacob's 2. Kompanie of Gebirgsjäger-Regiment 143, now dug in at the railway crossing after its wide outflanking movement. A Bren gun carrier swung into the attack at high speed but was quickly knocked out by an anti-tank rifle. This brought the rest of the convoy to a halt, the troops piling out and taking cover on either side of the road before returning fire. Two Bren gun carriers then swung onto the railway line to the south-east and tried to crash the roadblock from that direction but were unable to break through. Next, a 21st Battalion carrier rushed the road block with all Bren guns firing but was hit by a mortar bomb, the explosion lifting it off the road and into some boggy ground. When its crew attempted to drive it out, it became bellied on a rock and was abandoned. With this the attack collapsed and 30 Australians came forward to surrender, the rest making their escape across the fields to the south-east leaving some eight to ten dead and a further 20 wounded.

For a short time, further back, confusion reigned in the main column as they watched the tracer lighting up sky ahead. Some men decided to make a break for it on their own until order was restored. Eventually the column set off again towards a side track off the main road that an officer from the Divisional Cavalry thought might be a possible escape route. While moving gingerly forward towards the conflagration ahead, they came across a Greek peasant on the side of the road. After a short discussion he led them a few hundred metres further on to the start of the track they had been seeking. This soon turned into little more than a rutted cart track among the reeds and mud, and several trucks got stuck and had to be towed out by the carriers. Two Divisional Cavalry armoured cars also overturned, while one of the Australian carriers got mired in the mud and had to be destroyed. To make matters worse, at one point some drivers turned their headlights on, drawing fire from the Gebirgsjäger back at the railway crossing, until at last the lights were extinguished. The column eventually reached the main road, the New Zealanders turning left towards Volos and the Australians swinging back towards the main road to Lamia. The last of the column cleared the track around 4 a.m.

While Balck's men slept, the evacuation of W Force continued apace. By 1.30 a.m. on April 19 the last elements of the 6th NZ Brigade passed through Larissa, Savige Force clearing the town two and a half hours later. The final act saw the demolition of the two bridges over the Pineios at Larissa, first to go being the concrete bridge on the northern branch of the river. When the old stone bridge was demolished it went off in a spectacular fashion, the explosion blowing out windows in houses 25 blocks away.

AFTERMATH (April 19-22)

AT 3.50 A.M. ON THE morning of April 19 Oberst Balck requested an air drop of 3.7cm and 5cm high-explosive shells but this was denied because of a lack of suitable containers. Instead he was told the air force would look for a suitable landing ground for their Ju 52 transport aircraft. With this option gone, the battlegroup set off at 5 a.m., the remaining tanks on the road accompanied by the 7. Kompanie of Schützen-Regiment 304 to the right of the railway line and the 8. Kompanie to the left. They drove into Larissa at 6.15 a.m., a few hours ahead of the leading mountain troops, only to find the Anzacs long since departed and both bridges over the Pineios river destroyed. Worse still, Oberstleutnant Decker's medium tanks soon ground to a halt as they ran out of petrol. Despite orders not to proceed south of Larissa, he sent all his light PzKpfw IIs in that direction, in a desperate bid to overrun the enemy, but they were brought to a halt 40 kilometres south of the town, their fuel tanks dry. They had seen no enemy, only abandoned trucks and lorries on the road and deserted supply dumps here and there.

Of Kampfgruppe Koelitz there was no sign. In fact Oberst Koelitz had problems of his own. After struggling through demolitions left behind by the 6th NZ Brigade, his battlegroup reached Tyrnavos, 20 kilometres north-west of Larissa, at 9 a.m. that morning only to discover that the bridge over the Titarisios river, a tributary of the Pineios, had been blown. Working downstream from the bridge and weir, they discovered a place where the river could be forded and continued to push tanks and vehicles across it until 1.25 p.m. when it became impassable. At this point their advance came to an end, with no choice but to wait till their logistical train arrived. Further north, Panzer-Aufklärungs-Abteilung 5 had to set up camp north of Elasson, due to the road now being clogged by elements of the 9. Panzer-Division.

Back in Larissa, it did not take long for Balck's men to find the stocks of food left behind by W Force but they did not discover the British petrol dump until midday, by which time it was too late to follow up the Anzacs. In the end, their requested ammunition had to be flown into the airfield at Larissa. Taking stock, the final assessment of losses of the I. Abteilung of Panzer-Regiment 3 over the last four days revealed that they had lost 36 tanks (three PzKpfw IIs and one PzKpfw III swamped in the river; three PzKpfw IIs, 12 PzKpfw IIIs and two PzKpfw IVs with damage requiring three to eight days to repair; ten PzKpfw IIs and three PzKpfw IIIs knocked out by anti-tank guns or artillery

Balck's panzers reached Larissa on the morning of April 19 but were by then so short of fuel that the medium tanks ran out of petrol. Only the PzKpfw IIs of Hauptmann von Boxberg's 1. Kompanie and Oberleutnant Eckard von Nostitz-Wallwitz's 2. Kompanie still had some fuel in their tanks and were able to carry on but they too ran out 40 kilometres further south. Here one of them is seen passing through the town. (Jeffrey Plowman Collection)

and of questionable reparability, and two PzKpfw IVs destroyed by mines). Personnel losses of the battalion amounted to four dead and 37 wounded.

The leading elements of the 6. Gebirgs-Division reached Larissa around 10 a.m., Gebirgsjäger-Regiment 143 bivouacking inside the town, while Gebirgsjäger-Regiment 141 took up defensive positions outside. Like Balck's battlegroup they found vast stocks of food, from which it was possible to issue abundant portions to the division as they had received no regular rations since April 10.

Poised as the Germans were to strike further south from Larissa, limited progress was made that day, despite an order issued at 3.30 p.m. by Generalfeldmarschall List, the 12. Armee commander, for Böhme's XVIII. Gebirgs-Korps to advance on Volos and Stumme's XXXX. Armee-Korps to drive south towards Lamia. Böhme responded by ordering the 6. Gebirgs-Division to continue the advance south but nothing came of this as the division commander, Generalmajor Schörner, chose to declare April 20 a rest day for his exhausted troops. Stumme instructed the 5. Panzer-Division to take over the advance on Lamia but it soon became apparent that this was not possible as they had yet to reach the Thessaly plain.

Due to a major earthquake, which had hit the town on March 1, 1941, and extensive bombing by the Luftwaffe, few original buildings remain in Larissa today. The Kampfgruppe probably used Georgiadou Street, the only one wide enough to correspond to the one in the wartime photo and feeding into the town from the road to the Pineios gorge. This approximate comparison was taken opposite the citadel next to the Metropolitan Church of Agios Achillós. (Jeffrey Plowman)

Thus free from pursuit, though under constant Luftwaffe attack, the Anzacs continued their flight south, the Australians and the 26th NZ Battalion moving towards Lamia. The rest of the 6th NZ Brigade and the NZ Divisional Cavalry swung south-eastwards to Volos, reaching it that morning and establishing a blocking position there. They were joined towards midday by stragglers from the 21st NZ and 2/2nd Australian Battalions, the blocking force pulling out later that evening when it became apparent that no more were coming.

Any plans by Kampfgruppe Balck to follow up that day were also hampered by the fact that their logistical support system was in a mess. While they had managed to resurrect the ferry at Rapsani, the tunnel at Platamon was still a problem. After part of the roof had collapsed the previous day, they had, after a strenuous effort, managed to open it up on the evening of the 19th. Then to their dismay it collapsed less than half an hour later, with no clear idea of how long it would take to complete repairs. Now their only option was to continue using the saddle track and deal with all the difficulties associated with that.

Further towards the city centre there was an old stone road bridge over the southern channel of the Pineios river. In anticipation of the Germans' arrival, engineers of Nos. 2 and 3 Sections of 19th (Army Troops) Company, NZE had prepared all bridges in town for demolition. The ones assigned to this span worked intensively on preparing it for demolition over several days, opening up four-metre-long holes in the solid walls of the six arches and filling these with gelignite and ammonial. When they set these off in the early hours of April 19, the resulting explosion not only destroyed the bridge but blew out windows as far as 25 streets away. This only added to the damage already done by the earthquake and the heavy Luftwaffe bombing.

The Germans later erected this wooden replacement for the part of the bridge wrecked by the New Zealand engineers. When they departed from Greece in October 1944, they blew it up again.

Today two bridges cross the Pineios at this point, one a four-lane span for motor vehicles allowing for traffic in both directions on Grigoriou Lampraki Street, and immediately next to it (in the foreground) a smaller one for pedestrian traffic.
(Jeffrey Plowman)

A PzKpfw II and other vehicles en route to reinforce Kampfgruppe Balck at Larissa on April 19. (USNA StM 145-13)

Looking north on the N1 Makrikhori to Larissa road today. The snow-capped peak in the distance, obscured by dust in the wartime image, is Mount Ossa. (Google)

Also moving up was this a PzKpfw I mit Abwurfvorrichtung ('with charge-laying device'). It was a Panzer I Ausf. B fitted with a mechanism on the back to place an explosive load on obstacles. The explosives were ignited by a time fuze. A second vehicle of this type can be seen further down the column. Both belonged to Panzer-Pionier-Bataillon 38, which had ten such vehicles. (Early prototypes were known as Ladungsleger 1). (USNA StM 145-14)

Larissa lies on the east bank of the Pineios, so Kampfgruppe Balck did not need to cross the river to gain entry into the town. However this was different for Kampfgruppe Koelitz, the other half of the 2. Panzer-Division, which was advancing on the town from the north-west. The New Zealand engineers assigned to this concrete road bridge over the main arm of the river had found some explosives in a dump but considered these insufficient so they acquired two bombs from the airfield, wiring up one at each end of the bridge. They waited until the New Zealand Divisional Cavalry had passed through in the early hours of April 19 and then set off the charges. When the Germans reached Larissa, they put captured Anzac soldiers (including an Australian with his distinctive slouch hat) to work to prepare the way for a temporary bridge. (Mike Smythe Collection)

Engineers of Panzer-Pionier-Bataillon 38 and Brücken-Kolonne 1/410 reached Larissa late on the 20th and quickly started work on a pontoon bridge beside the broken road bridge.

Today, a modern highway bridge crosses the river at this point. (Jeffrey Plowman)

Meanwhile, the supply situation for the 2. Panzer-Division remained problematic. Back at Platamon, the German engineers were still experiencing problems with opening the railway tunnel underneath the ridge for traffic. On April 18, after two days of work, they managed to open it, allowing some vehicles through, but at midday part of the roof collapsed, again halting all movement. Another 31 hours on, at 7.15 p.m. on April 19, Panzer-Pionier-Bataillon 38 reported the tunnel clear again but part of the roof fell in a second time less than half an hour later, closing the tunnel for an indeterminate period and forcing the Germans back to using the saddle track. Among the units stranded before the tunnel were parts of the divisional bridging column, elements of Panzerjäger-Abteilung 38, of Artillerie-Regiment 74, of schwere Infanterie-Geschütz-Kompanie 703 and most of the supply column of Schützen-Regiment 304. Once finally re-opened, the tunnel provided an easier route past Platamon ridge for horse-drawn wagons such as this. (Greece in WWII Archives)

After the war, the Greeks added a concrete extension over the railway tracks to protect it from falling rock. After the new high-speed line was opened in 2004, the tracks lay abandoned for a time and were then largely concreted over, and the tunnel extension was turned into the Gallaria Beach Bar. To show patrons the original purpose of the structure, the bar owners left a short section of track uncovered at the entrance. The German guard tower was also retained. (During their occupation of Greece, the Germans built numerous such towers and pillboxes along the vital Salonika to Athens railway line to protect it against sabotage and attacks by partisans). (Google)

German vehicles exiting the tunnel at its southern end. (Franz Steinzer)

Since the war, the only changes are a new concrete portal and the addition of an abutment. Today, the tunnel provides easy access to the Gallaria Beach Bar from this side of the ridge. Not far from here stands another of the guard towers built by the Germans in 1943. (Jeffrey Plowman)

Further south, in the Pineios gorge, the supply situation had also improved. Here, the German engineers managed to get the ferry, which the New Zealanders had sunk on the 16th, operational again, as evidenced by this picture taken from the north bank. Strangely enough, the motorcyclists seem to be disembarking, i.e. returning to their own side of the river. The abutment in the background represents the start the Greeks had made to build a bridge here.
(Greece in WWII Archives)

Later engineers of Brücken-Kolonnen 1/413 and 1/415 assembled a floating pontoon bridge at this point. It can be seen on the far left, beside the abutment. The view is looking west, into the Pineios gorge.
(George Handrinos)

Looking westwards down the present-day Athens to Thessaloniki highway. The distinctive peak on the other side of the gorge provides the link with the past. The concrete abutment was located about midway between the present-day bridge leading into the gorge and the Rapsani railway station. (Google)

Kampfgruppe Koelitz, the western prong of the 2. Panzer-Division's drive on Larissa, reached the town of Tyrnavos, 20 kilometres north-west of Larissa, on the morning of April 19 but found the bridge over the Titarisios river there destroyed by New Zealand engineers. (Jeffrey Plowman Collection)

The bridge has been carefully restored but the presence of a Greek military camp close to its southern end today prevents an exact match. This comparison is taken from the other side of the bridge ramp, looking north-west instead of north-east. (Google)

Though they had plenty of food at Larissa there was, apparently, not enough petrol to mobilise all of Balck's panzers. At least the battlegroup had not been idle, turning their attention to recovering what tanks they could from the battleground between the gorge and Makrikhori, this effort bringing its tank strength up to 40 by the end of the day. Orders were sent to the division's engineer battalions to build bridges over the Pineios river at Larissa and for Kampfgruppe Koelitz to push a bridge over the Titarisios river at Tyrnavos. Despite all this, Balck was keen to push on soon with something and around 4 p.m. had assembled a scratch force consisting of the 1. Kompanie of Panzerjäger-Abteilung 38 and one platoon from the 6. Kompanie of Schützen-Regiment 304 with orders to reconnoitre southwards. This force reached Domokos around midday on April 20 and some two hours later ran into the Australian blocking force located below the pass to Lamia,

Downstream of the bridge and its associated weir the Germans found a place where the river could be forded. However, by early afternoon the passage of vehicles had turned the crossing point into a quagmire, halting further advance of Kampfgruppe Koelitz until the river could be bridged. These Panzer IIIs belong to the II. Abteilung of Panzer-Regiment 3. Only the tanks of its 5. Kompanie managed to cross the river and reach Larissa that day. (USNA StP 148-28)

The range of hills behind the town pinpoints the ford as being about midway between the old Tyrnavos to Larissa road and the modern Elasson to Larissa highway that today skirts the town on its eastern side. The stone arched bridge can be seen behind the utility pole. (Google)

now reduced to a couple of companies with some anti- tank guns, artillery and the five remaining A13 Cruiser tanks from the British 1st Armoured Brigade HQ Squadron. In the ensuing engagement one A13 was hit and set on fire, the Australians claiming a German armoured car disabled, while a PzKpfw II was hit several times and damaged but managed to withdraw successfully.

That same day, April 20, forward elements of the 9. Panzer-Division reached Tyrnavos (OL 2116). They found Kampfgruppe Koelitz already there,

When the 5. Kompanie reached Larissa at noon of April 19, the pontoon bridge that the German engineers had started building over the Pineios there (see page 126) was not yet ready so troops were initially transported across by way of a pontoon ferry, here watched by General der Kavallerie Georg Stumme, the commander of the XXXX. Armee-Korps. (USNA StP 149-03)

the force still waiting for completion of a bridge over the Titarisios. Further to the west, the 5. Panzer-Division entered onto the plain of Thessaly, after driving into Kalabaka the previous evening. Bypassing Larissa, the division set off on the more-direct route to Domokos until a heavy thunderstorm turned the road into a quagmire that slowed their progress even more. By the time they reached the main road between Pharsala and Domokos it was clogged by other traffic also heading south. To add to their woes, the LSSAH, ordered to move onto the road they had just traversed, cut them off from their logistical train. At this point their quartermaster officer ordered them to live off the land and seek out petrol supplies from wherever they could. Nevertheless, leading elements of the division did eventually manage to get through the logjam and reach Domokos around midday. Here they were joined that evening by the small combat group from Panzerjäger-Abteilung 38 and Schützen-Regiment 304, the latter on their way back from the foot of the pass over to Lamia.

By the evening of April 20 the Anzacs had completed their withdrawal behind the Sperchios river, which runs west to east just below Lamia, with the 5th NZ Brigade holding a defensive position on the hills beyond. Further

The pontoon bridge was finally completed at 12.30 p.m. on the 21st, allowing the 5. Kompanie to cross over to the east bank, this PzKpfw III among them. With the bridge at Tyrnavos completed at 3.30 p.m. on the 22nd, the rest of Kampfgruppe Koelitz was then able to join up with Kampfgruppe Balck, reuniting the two tank battalions of Panzer-Regiment 3. That evening, Balck could report that he had 94 operational tanks (down from the 116 he had started the invasion with). (Jeffrey Plowman Collection)

Many more tanks reached Larissa later, part of the 9. Panzer-Division passing through the town to join the southward drive on Athens. Here PzKpfw IIIs from that division's Panzer-Regiment 33 cross the pontoon bridge on April 26. (Jeffrey Plowman Collection)

The lone pier in the river just downstream from today's highway bridge might well be a remnant of the old concrete span. (Ioannis Delfos)

For their escape south from Larissa the 26th NZ Battalion was divided into two parties, one travelling by rail and the other by trucks. The latter followed the route allocated to Australian troops, via Domokos and Lamia. The column came under attack from Stuka dive-bombers several times on the morning of April 19, first at the foot of the Domokos Pass and then after clearing Domokos itself. During the latter attack someone had the presence of mind to take a photo as he and his fellow soldiers abandoned their truck. Note the A10 Cruiser tank in the background. (ATL DA-03563)

back, in reserve, were the 4th and 6th NZ Brigades and over to their left two battalions from the 19th Australian Brigade in blocking position at the Brallos Pass, extending this as more units came in from Lamia. On the night of April 20/21, based on a belief that German troops had entered Lamia, all the bridges over the Sperchios were demolished. This proved to be timely as an Ultra intercept (OL 2129) indicated that German intentions for the next day were to push on through Lamia towards Athens, though they were expecting to meet resistance at Thermopylae.

On April 21 the 6th NZ Brigade moved into position around Thermopylae, with the 25th NZ Battalion (Lieutenant-Colonel Allan Wilder) occupying the area north of Molos. Just in time it would appear because that afternoon advance elements of Panzer-Aufklärungs-Abteilung 8 from the 5. Panzer-Division reached Lamia, sending out three patrols towards the Sperchios river. While two of these reported all the bridges blown, contact was lost with the third. In fact the two motorcyclists from the latter were cut down by fire from the 23rd NZ Battalion Carrier Platoon when they rode up to the demolished bridge, one being killed and the other captured. Around 9 p.m. elements of Kradschützen-Bataillon 55 (Oberstleutnant Hans Schacke) from the 5. Panzer-Division reached Lamia after an exhausting march over the pass. That evening there were further adjustments to the New Zealand

The A10, from No. 1 Troop of A Squadron of the 3rd Royal Tanks, was commanded by Lieutenant Robert Crisp. After it had cleared the Domokos Pass, Crisp and his crew pulled off the road for some rest and maintenance but unfortunately a track pin snapped in the rough ground, forcing them to abandon the vehicle. It was in fact Crisp's third loss of a tank through mechanical failure within five days (see pages 34-35 and 72-73). The immobilised tank suffered further damage during the Stuka attack. Passing German soldiers later daubed the words 'No overtaking before Lamia' on the turret and 'England's last hope' on the track guard. (Robert Gregory Collection)

The ridgeline in the distance provides a perfect comparison for both photos. The view is looking south-east in the middle of the plain, near the road turnoff to the village of Xiniada. (Google)

The other two battalions from the 6th NZ Brigade – the 24th and 25th Battalions – proceeded on to Volos under orders to establish a rearguard there. They arrived on the morning of April 19, being joined a few hours later by stragglers from the 21st NZ and 2/2nd Australian Battalions. The New Zealanders pulled out that evening after it became clear that no more escapees were coming. This Universal Carrier Mk I and Marmon-Herrington Mk II armoured car were pictured on the road south from Volos most probably that same day. (Frank Horton)

The headland and the hills beyond help to pinpoint the spot to the coastal road south-west of Volos, some three kilometres before reaching the town of Nea Anchialos. (Google)

positions when the 19th Battalion was sent back to reconnoitre a defensive position in the Delphi Pass to cover a possible breakthrough from the west.

On the morning of April 22, with a bridge over the Titarisios river at Tyrnavos finally complete, Kampfgruppe Koelitz was at last able to move forward, Panzer-Regiment 3 reporting a tank strength of 94 following their link-up with Balck's force that afternoon.

Around that same time, 90 kilometres further south, Kradschützen-Bataillon 55 crossed the Sperchios river near the village of Kostalexis, south-west of Lamia, and pushed into the hills towards Brallos. Here they ran up against the main Australian position and were forced to halt and dig in, a situation not helped by the supply situation hampering the aircraft of the VIII. Fliegerkorps to provide support (OL 2143).

During the withdrawal of Savige Force from Larissa to Lamia on April 19, one of the A13 tanks of the British 1st Armoured Brigade Headquarters Squadron had to be abandoned, apparently after becoming stuck in a swamp off the main road. (Aris Kosionidis)

All seven A13s of the Brigade Headquarters Protective Troop had been sent over to the New Zealand Division in exchange for two troops of armoured cars from the NZ Divisional Cavalry. T-18153 was one of the seven. (Mike Smythe Collection)

It came to grief some five kilometres south-west of Pharsala, just before reaching the village of Vrisia, visible on the far right. The wetland is still very much in existence. (Google)

On April 20, a rearguard was established at the foot of the Furka Pass leading over to Lamia with a company each from the 2/6th and 2/7th Australian Battalions, eight anti-tank guns from the 31st Battery of the 7th NZ Anti-Tank Regiment, some Vickers machine guns from the 2/1st Australian MG Battalion, a few armoured cars from the NZ Divisional Cavalry and the five remaining A13s from the 1st Armoured Brigade Headquarters Squadron. That afternoon, the force came under attack from a reconnaissance force sent out by the 2. Panzer-Division consisting of the 1. Kompanie of Panzerjäger-Abteilung 38 and a platoon from the 6. Kompanie of Schützen-Regiment 304. The only significant loss was this A13 (T-18151) that caught fire after being hit. (Robert Gregory Collection)

It was knocked out just where the road starts to ascend the pass. (Google)

After the Germans were driven off, the rearguard withdrew over the pass. During this move, two of the A13s broke down and had to be abandoned, among them T-7035. (Robert Gregory Collection)

The same spot near the top of the pass, looking back down towards the Domokos plain. (Google)

On April 23, a German convoy halted at practically the same spot while waiting for a detour to be made around the site of a road demolition. (USNA StM 157-07)

German troops from the 5. Panzer-Division finally entered Lamia on the afternoon of April 23. Here a SdKfz 231 eight-wheeled heavy armoured reconnaissance car from its Panzer-Aufklärungs-Abteilung 8 drives into a small square. (USNA StM 157-15)

The same square – Plateia Eleitherias (Freedom Square) – today with Sklivaniotu Street on the left. The building at far right nowadays houses the Consulate of Austria. (Google)

EVACUATION (April 23-May 1)

THE ARRIVAL OF THE Anzacs at the Thermopylae Line marked a turning point for W Force. General Wilson's revised plan had been to defend southern Greece from here but now it was becoming apparent that this was no longer realistic. As early as April 13, with the German entry into Belgrade, it had become clear to Middle East Command in Cairo that the Balkan front was likely to collapse. During a visit to Athens between April 11 and 13 General Wavell, the Commander-in-Chief of Middle East Command, had warned Wilson that no more reinforcements could be sent. At the same time he authorised Lieutenant-Colonel Francis de Guingand, a member of his Joint Planning Staff, to prepare some plans for an evacuation. Two days later Wavell, Admiral Cunningham, the Commander-in-Chief of the Mediterranean Fleet, and Air Chief Marshall Longmore, Wavell's air force commander, came to the painful conclusion that they had to withdraw W Force from Greece. In fact on April 16 the Greek Army commander, General Papagos, also suggested the same thing to Wilson, prompting the latter to contact Middle East Command about this that day. This led to the dispatch of Rear-Admiral Harold Baillie-Grohman to Greece on April 17 with orders to begin preparations for an evacuation. This resulted in the formation of a joint planning staff in Athens that day, whose first response was to send out parties to look for suitable beaches.

While Churchill concurred with this, he was also adamant that consent to this course of action should be obtained from the Greek government. Nevertheless, he was still confident that Greece could be held, even if only at the Thermopylae Line. Wilson, however, opined that his force could not fight on for another month and would certainly not be able to hold the Thermopylae position. Wavell was more buoyant and felt that if W Force could maintain that position there was no reason to hasten the evacuation and continued to hold this view after flying to Greece on April 19. Unfortunately, the British soon found out that the Greek government was in disarray. The Greek Prime Minister, Koryzis, committed suicide on April 18 after confessing to the reigning Greek monarch, King George II, that he had failed him in defending Greece, leaving the King no choice but to take over as head of government. Wilson initiated discussions with the King and General Papagos at which it was decided that the best option was to withdraw W Force from Greece, starting on the night of April 28/29.

On April 24, the 5. Panzer-Division launched its attack on the Thermopylae Line, the main thrust being made towards the little town of Molos by the 19 tanks of the 1. Kompanie of Panzer-Regiment 31 supported by advance elements of the 72. Infanterie-Division. In the ensuing drive along the coastal road artillery fire forced the infantry to take cover, leaving the tanks to carry on alone, 12 of them ultimately being knocked out by New Zealand artillery and anti-tank guns. (Lee Archer)

The same spot today. The view is looking westwards back towards the town of Thermopylae. (Google)

Map of southern Greece showing the battle sites at Thermopylae – the Brallos Pass and Molos – in the north and the embarkation beaches used during the evacuation in the south: Rafina [1] and Porto Rafti [2] on the eastern coast of Attica, Megara [3] in West Attica and Navplion [4], Monemvasia [5] and Kalamata [6] in the Peloponnese. (British Official History)

A further deterioration in the situation, however, forced a change in these plans. Following the diversion of the LSSAH from Grevena to Ioaninna to isolate the Greek forces west of the Pindus mountains, Lieutenant-General Georgios Tsolakoglou, commander of the Greek III Army Corps, and certain other senior officers deposed their Army commander, Lieutenant-General Ioannis Pitsikas. Tsolakoglou then opened negotiations on April 20 with SS-Obergruppenführer Sepp Dietrich, commander of the LSSAH, at Larissa, signing a surrender protocol that same day, though, in deference to their Italian allies, Generalfeldmarschall List cancelled this, allowing a formal surrender to be made to the Italians two days later.

The British learned of this on April 21 through an Ultra intercept (OL 2128): 'Commander of an unidentified Greek Army believed ready to capitulate'. For the British this was the final straw as the Thermopylae Line could now be outflanked from the west and was no longer tenable as a defensive position. On his return from Blamey's headquarters that day Wavell met with the Greek King and the new Prime Minister, Emmanouil

Despite being on their way to evacuation beaches at Porto Rafti and Rafina, these trucks from the 5th NZ Field Regiment passing through Athens on Anzac Day, April 25, received an enthusiastic reception from the local civilians. (Ivan Collins via Ian Collins)

The trucks were on Stadiou Street, just short of its intersection with Voukourestiou Street (on the left) and travelling in a south-easterly direction. This suggests that the convoy was on its way to the evacuation beaches, and not being welcomed after their arrival in March as stated in some publications on the Greek campaign. (Antonis Voutsinos)

Tsouderos. Now in no doubt that the date of the evacuation had to be brought forward, he told Wilson that he was free to choose the date. Then news came through that the Greek armies in Epirus had surrendered, so the start date was moved forward to April 24/25. Thus Operation 'Demon' was born. At least they could take comfort from one thing, an Ultra intercept (OL 2146) on April 23 stating that an attack on Thermopylae 'with stronger forces' was not expected before April 24.

At that point things began to move quickly. In Alexandria the Royal Navy began assembling an evacuation fleet under the command of Vice Admiral Sir Henry Pridham-Wippell. As finally configured it included four cruisers, three anti-aircraft cruisers, 20 destroyers, two infantry assault ships and 19 medium-sized troopships. In the meantime in Greece, each division withdrew one brigade group, the 19th Australian Brigade going to Megara, a port town 40 kilometres west of Athens, and the 5th NZ Brigade to Rafina and Porto Rafti, located east and south-east of Athens respectively, while the 4th NZ Brigade took up another rearguard position at Kriekouki, 80 kilometres south of Thermopylae and 25 kilometres north-west of Athens. That night, after an attack on the airfield at Argos in the Peloponnese, the last five Hurricanes of the RAF flew out of Greece, leaving W Force totally without air cover. Blamey and some of his staff were also flown out by Sunderland flying boat.

On April 24, the Germans finally launched their attack on the Thermopylae Line. This began in the morning with an assault by Kradschützen-Bataillon 55 on the 2/11th Australian Battalion in the Brallos Pass, one that was beaten off almost as soon as it started. That afternoon they turned their attention to the coastal road, tanks from the 1. Kompanie (Hauptmann Wilhelm Prinz von Schönburg-Waldenburg) of the I. Abteilung of Panzer-Regiment 31 (Oberstleutnant Gustav Freiherr von Bodenhausen) from the 5. Panzer-Division linking up with advance elements of Aufklärungs-Abteilung 112. With little time to coordinate the attack, 19 panzers set off in single file down the road only to see their supporting infantry forced to the ground by heavy artillery fire. Undeterred, the tanks carried on alone but within minutes of running into the New Zealand guns 12 of them were knocked out, four or five on fire. The rest beat a hasty retreat. Above them the 72. Infanterie-Division (General der Infanterie Franz Mattenklott) made steady progress against the 25th NZ Battalion, threatening to encircle the battalion, and forcing it to withdraw. This left the gun crews down on the road no choice but to hold on until nightfall when they pulled out. Luckily for them, the Germans did not follow up immediately, only entering Molos in the early hours of the following morning.

After that the evacuation began in earnest, a total of 5,700 troops, including the 5th NZ Brigade, were successfully uplifted from Porto Rafti that night, while a further 6,685 men and women were rescued at Navplion in the Peloponnese, disturbed there only by the grounding of the MV *Ulster Prince* in the harbour. It was finally destroyed the next day by dive-bombers.

On April 26, in a bold airborne coup de main, paratroopers and glidermen from Fallschirmjäger-Regiment 2 captured the bridge over the Corinth Canal and rendered it safe by the removal of the explosive charges on it, only to see it blow up in their faces after a stray round struck the explosives they had piled up in the centre. This sign on the north bank directs traffic to a pontoon bridge built later by the Germans at the western end of the canal. (Mike Smythe Collection)

Of the divisional commanders, Major-General Mackay was also ordered to leave and flew out that night. Freyberg, unwilling to leave when his troops were under a major attack, stayed on.

On April 25, because of the departure of the RAF and the loss of some ships, there was a change in plans, with some more troops now to be evacuated from the Peloponnese. Extending the 4th NZ Brigade's defence of Kriekouki by a day, the 16th and 17th Australian Brigades were moved down to Argos and the 6th NZ Brigade to Tripolis. Corinth, at the entrance to the Peloponnese, was also to be reinforced, some troops passing through being called aside to bolster its defences around the Corinth Canal bridge. That night, 5,900 men were taken off from Megara, among them the 19th Australian Brigade.

Corinth did not stay in W Force hands for long, the bridge over the deep-cut canal being captured by a German parachute and glider assault on April 26, only to be destroyed moments after, cutting W Force in two. That night, the British 1st Armoured Brigade and the NZ Divisional Cavalry – 8,203 men in all – were evacuated from Porto Rafti and Rafina, and 8,650 men from the 16th and 17th Australian Brigades from Kalamata, the port on the south-eastern shore of the Peloponnese. Another 4,527 troops were also uplifted from Navplion and Tolos, a small village six kilometres south of there, though some 900 died when the Dutch transport *Slamat* and two of its rescue ships, the destroyers *Diamond* and *Wryneck*, were sunk by the Luftwaffe. Wilson, himself, was flown out from Myloi that night by Sunderland flying boat, after placing Freyberg in charge of the rest of the evacuation.

By the time they got within striking distance of Athens the Germans seemed more interested in seeing who could reach the Greek capital first, rather than preventing the Anzacs from escaping. First to enter the city on the morning of April 27 was a platoon of motorcycle troops from Gebirgs-Panzerjäger-Abteilung 47 of the 6. Gebirgs-Division, which crossed the city boundaries city at 8.14 a.m., followed six minutes later by the 8. Kompanie of Regiment z.b.V. 800 'Brandenburg'. They immediately proceeded to the Acropolis, the great outcrop of rock that towers over the inner city, and raised the swastika flag there as a token of their conquest. The short ceremony was covered by several Wehrmacht photographers, this shot being taken by Bildberichter Bauer from Propaganda-Kompanie 690. (BA Bild 101I-165-419-19A)

The flag was raised at the mast that stands on the platform at the eastern end of the Acropolis. The Parthenon, the central and most famous of the ancient temples on the rock, remains to pinpoint the comparison.

On the morning of April 27 German troops finally entered Athens, the 5. Panzer-Division setting off towards Corinth, brushing past outer elements of the 4th NZ Brigade in the process. That night 3,840 men of the brigade group were uplifted from Porto Rafti. Not so lucky were the troops at Tolos-Navplion, their rearguard being overrun, this forcing the rest south to Kalamata.

The last major evacuation occurred on the night of April 28/29 when 4,320 men of the 6th NZ Brigade Group were evacuated from Monemvasia at the south-eastern tip of the Peloponnese, leaving some 8,000 men at Kalamata further west. Unfortunately, their rescue on the night of April 29/30 was confounded by the last-minute arrival of the 5. Panzer-Division. The fighting that developed along the waterfront was enough to discourage

These SdKfz 231 eight-wheeled heavy armoured cars from Panzer-Aufklärungs-Abteilung 8 from the 5. Panzer-Division arrived in Athens some time afterwards. (USNA StM 149-37)

They stood parked in front of the Grande Bretagne Hotel on Panepistimiou Street, where Generalfeldmarschall Wilhelm List, the commander of the 12. Armee, had by then set up his headquarters. (Google)

On April 27, after investigating reports of English troops abandoning vehicles and fleeing to the coast, the 5. Panzer-Division swung away from the Anzac evacuation beaches at Rafina and Porto Rafti and set off westwards towards Corinth. (Greece in WWII Archives)

the ships offshore from closing in on the harbour, even though a counter-attack by some Anzac soldiers managed to restore control of the town temporarily. The evacuation force eventually left without attempting to recover anyone. Another attempt was made later that night by some ships sent from Crete but it only managed to uplift 332. Thus ended Operation 'Demon'.

The same spot on the old coastal road just past Megara. (Google)

In the end, out of the 62,612 troops sent to Greece, a total of 903 were killed, 1,250 wounded and 13,958 taken prisoner. Among those left behind were 1,500 Yugoslav troops, the New Zealand Replacement Battalion and unarmed and leaderless base troops. Total losses of equipment amounted to 104 tanks, 28 armoured cars, 250 carriers, 40 anti-aircraft guns, 192 field guns, 164 anti-tank guns, approximately 8,000 transport vehicles and 209 aircraft. In addition to this, 26 ships were sunk during the evacuation. In contrast, the Germans claimed losses of 1,160 dead, 3,755 wounded and 365 missing.

With the pontoon bridge over the Corinth canal in place, the 5. Panzer-Division was able to rapidly occupy the Peloponnese but not before a sizeable body of W Force troops had been evacuated. Here a truck towing an 8.8cm Flak 36 anti-aircraft gun crosses over the bridge, a so-called Kriegsbrücke aus B-Gerät with a capacity of 16 tonnes. (USNA StM 158-21)

After spending a day hiding from aerial observation, on April 28 troops from the 6th NZ Brigade began moving down to their evacuation beach at Monemvasia, at the south-eastern tip of the Peloponnese. All were taken off that night, along with some personnel from the 3rd Royal Tanks, some 4,320 men in total. Here a few of them make their way to the beach. (Frank Keyes)

The same stretch of coastline today. The town of Monemvasia is actually located on the other side of the promontory on the left, the isthmus connecting it to the mainland now obscured by the new houses ahead. (Nikos Stavropoulos)

Luckily for the New Zealanders, the Germans were unaware of their presence at Monemvasia, the 5. Panzer-Division instead striking out for Kalamata where a larger force lay. This column of Krupp-Protze light trucks from the division was pictured on April 30. (USNA StP 151-01)

After successfully evacuating 8,650 men from Kalamata on the night of April 26/27, another attempt was made on the night of April 29/30 to extract the rest but this was interrupted by the entry of the 5. Panzer-Division into the town. Disturbed after the fighting had spread along the quay, the evacuating ships departed, leaving nearly 8,000 men behind. Here a group of them is being marched through town on their way to prisoner-of-war camps in Germany. (Greece in WWII Archives)

Kalamata is the capital and central port of Messinia prefect and has changed a lot since the war but fortunately the building behind the POW column, on Navarinou Road along the waterfront, is still there. Rising in the background is Mount Kalthio. (Google)

THE SINKING OF A PANZER DIVISION (May 15-21)

FOLLOWING THE END OF hostilities in Greece on April 28, German attention turned to the extrication of its forces there, in particular their panzer divisions, and their return to Germany to bring them back up to strength for the invasion of the Soviet Union, scheduled to be launched on June 22. However, with the 5. Panzer-Division in the Peloponnese and the 2. Panzer-Division around Athens, getting them out was not going to be that easy. Not only had the retreating troops of the British and Commonwealth expeditionary force damaged the roads in their retreat but they had carried out a thorough set of demolitions on the rail network as well. In fact the line from Salonika (Thessaloniki) to the Yugoslav border could not be re-opened

German plans at the end of Operation 'Marita' called for the withdrawal of the 2. Panzer-Division to Germany where it was to re-equip in preparation for its deployment in Operation 'Barbarossa', the Axis invasion of the Soviet Union. As part of the division's return to Germany, its tracked and semi-tracked vehicles and associated equipment were to be shipped over from Patras in the Peloponnese to Taranto in Italy in two separate convoys, one on May 18 and another on May 21. During the second convoy, both cargo ships involved, the *Kybfels* and *Marburg*, hit mines that had been laid by the British minelayer HMS *Abdiel* the night before and sank with heavy losses of personnel and equipment, a total of 243 sailors and soldiers being killed and 355 guns and vehicles being lost. This makes the event one of the worst single-day losses suffered by a German panzer division during the war. This picture taken from an Italian aircraft shows the *Marburg* on fire. (Archivio Centrale dello Stato)

The Marburg was a 7,564-tonne four-masted passenger/cargo ship built by the Schichau F. Werft (Ferdinand Schichau) shipyard in Danzig (Gdansk) in 1928 and owned by the Norddeutscher Lloyd shipping company. Originally named *Saale*, she was renamed *Marburg* in 1938. Here she is docking at Patras to take aboard men and materiel of the 2. Panzer-Division. (Deutsches Historisches Museum)

The same waterfront beside the Othonos kai Amalias Boulevard, quite close to a small railway station. (Jeffrey Plowman)

The *Kybfels* was a 7,764-tonne cargo ship built by the Deutsche Schiff- und Maschinenbau AG (Deschimag) Weser in Bremen in 1937 and owned by the Hansa Bremen company.

until early in July 1941, along with the Pineios river bridge and the line from Salonika to Florina. The big problem was the four large bridges and viaducts in central Greece that had been destroyed during the final stages of the withdrawal of the Anzac Corps to Thermopylae. Three of these were restored to functionality in mid-May but the large viaduct of Papida was only made operational on March 28, 1942. This meant that all trains between Salonika and Athens terminated at Liankladi/Lamia and Brallos, the passengers and goods being transported by lorries between these two stations.

For the 2. Panzer-Division this resulted in a long journey by road up the coast to Split in Yugoslavia for its wheeled elements and thence by train for Germany, the first elements leaving Split on May 15 and 16. The tracked elements, however, were to be shipped over to Italy and thence to Germany, the departure point being the port of Patras on the north-western corner of the Peloponnese. As there was a limited amount of shipping available this was to take place in two stages, the first convoy consisting of the cargo ships SS *Kybfels* (Kapitän Schliemann), SS *Laura C* and the passenger/cargo ship MV *Marburg*. Onto these ships vehicles from the following units were loaded: Panzer-Regiment 3, Kradschützen-Bataillon 2, Panzerjäger-Abteilung 38, Panzer-Nachrichten-Abteilung 38, Panzer-Pionier-Bataillon 38 (without its bridging column), schwere Infanterie-Geschütz-Kompanie 703 and the 2. Kompanie of Maschinengewehr-Bataillon 47. This contingent, under the command of Oberst Balck, the commander of Panzer-Regiment 3, departed Patras on May 18, reaching Taranto the same

Priority for loading was given to the tanks of Panzer-Regiment 3, and they all went with the first shipment, which left Patras on May 18 and safely reached Taranto that same day. This PzKpfw IV – number 314 – belongs to the 3. Kompanie of the regiment's I. Abteilung.

Present to watch the loading were (L-R) Oberst Hermann Balck, commander of Panzer-Regiment 3; Oberleutnant Horst Rämsch, the regimental adjutant; Generalfeldmarschall Wilhelm List, commander of the 12. Armee; Oberstleutnant Karl Decker, commander of the regiment's I. Abteilung; Hauptmann Albrecht von Boxberg, commander of the regiment's 1. Kompanie, and Oberschirrmeister Büschel. (Franz Steinzer)

day. The following day *Kybfels* and *Marburg* returned to Patras and began loading the remaining vehicles of the division.

In the meantime on May 18, having received reports of a British submarine in the area, the Regia Marina (Italian Royal Navy) sent the submarine *Ciro Menotti* (Capitano di Corvetta Ugo Gelli) to patrol the area south of the island of Zakynthos. Around midnight the crew observed a dark shape heading eastwards at 15 knots. Just which ship this was is not clear but on the night of May 20/21 the British minelayer HMS *Abdiel* laid a field of 150 mines east of Akra Dhoukaton (Cape Doukato), the southern tip of Lefkada island. A few hours later the Italian gunboat *Pellegrino Matteucci* on its way to Patras blew up on a mine, followed sometime later by the Italian destroyer *Carlo Mirabello*, which was escorting a convoy.

Unfortunately, no word of this reached the 2. Panzer-Division at Patras, relations between the Italians and Germans being somewhat strained at the time, consequently consultation between them was practically non-existent. Though there were numerous ships of the Regia Marina in port, among them 12 destroyers and the light cruiser *Bari*, the Germans were informed that they would meet their two escorts once they had cleared the narrow passage

German crews inspecting their tanks in the hold of the *Kybfels*, these ones being PzKpfw IIs, some of which are from the 2. Kompanie. (Larry Te Koeti)

Also included in the shipments were these SdKfz 7 medium half-tracks. Vehicles of this type were in both convoys, however the writing on the back of this photo says '*Kybfels*, Patras, 16.05.41', indicating these particular ones went with the first shipment on May 18. (Larry Te Koeti)

between Akra Dhoukaton and the islands of Ithaca and Cephalonia. Thus on the morning of May 21 *Kybfels* and *Marburg* proceeded out of the harbour, having taken on board the second contingent, under the command of Major Arno Reinke (the commander of the I. Abteilung of Artillerie-Regiment 74). This comprised men and vehicles of Artillerie-Regiment 74, Panzer-Aufklärungs-Abteilung 5, Panzer-Pionier-Bataillon 38, Schützen-Regiment 2, Schützen-Regiment 304, schwere Infanterie-Geschütz-Kompanie 703, Sanitäts-Kompanie 2/82, the 1. Batterie of leichte Flak-Abteilung 76, and a small detachment of two vehicles and a trailer from Panzer-Regiment 3 and Schützen-Brigade 'Leibstandarte-SS Adolf Hitler'.

Around 10 p.m., having crossed the gulf of Patras and finally reached the open sea two kilometres to the south-east of Akra Dhoukaton, the *Kybfels*, in the lead, struck a mine, the impact point being in the vicinity of the bridge, the water column from the detonation also sending a waterspout up the level of the bridge. Filling it quickly with smoke, the explosion also tore away the cover of Hatch 3 and the ship began to take on water. The immediate response of the crew was to lower its lifeboats but they also threw a lot of life-rafts into the sea while it was still in motion. Taking evasive action, the *Kybfels* swung to starboard immediately, only to strike another mine amidships, followed a few minutes later by a third at the stern of the ship, causing her to list to

On the morning of May 21, the *Kybfels* and *Marburg* departed Patras with the second shipment, carrying 355 vehicles and 1,278 soldiers of the 2. Panzer-Division. Around 10 a.m., as they emerged from the narrow passage between Akra Dhoukaton and the islands of Ithaki and Cephalonia, both ships struck mines, that had been laid by the British minelayer HMS *Abdiel* the night before. (British Official History)

starboard and she started to sink. Following the first explosion, Kapitän Schliemann had ordered all to abandon ship, resulting in a flurry of activity on board as the crew and the 2. Panzer-Division troops took to the water. Within 15 minutes the ship had disappeared.

The *Marburg* suffered the same fate. Just after the *Kybfels* struck its first mine, *Marburg* passed it at full speed only to strike another mine on its starboard side and catch fire shortly afterwards. This soon spread along

The *Kybfels* sank within 15 minutes, leaving little time to lower lifeboats, but the *Marburg*, having caught fire after hitting two mines, stayed afloat for longer, allowing more time for rescue operations. This picture taken from an Italian aircraft shows the *Marburg* on fire. (Archivio Centrale dello Stato)

the upper deck to the anti-aircraft guns, the ammunition of which started to explode. Here too lifeboats were lowered and inflatable boats prepared. Unlike the *Kybfels*, the *Marburg* did not sink immediately and so the crew was able to lower the ropes and there was time to evacuate the ship in an orderly fashion. So much time in fact that some engineer soldiers on board insisted on finishing cooking and eating some meat they had purchased in Patras before embarking!

Within a short space of time many of the survivors in the lifeboats from the two ships were picked up by some Italian motor cutters and taken back to Patras. Those in the water were not so lucky, many of them floating in the sea for two and a half or three hours, some succumbing from exhaustion. The rest were eventually rescued by Greek fishermen from the island of Ithaca. On May 22 these were picked up by the Italians at the port of Physkardon and transported to either Argostoli, the main town in Cephalonia, or Same, where 56 of the dead were buried. All of the survivors were eventually reunited in Patras on May 25. On June 1 they were shipped through the Gulf of Corinth to Corinth itself and from there by truck to Salonika. Some seven days later, the last of the men reached Augsburg and the division itself.

In all, 633 men from the 2. Panzer-Division had embarked on the *Kybfels* and 645 on the *Marburg* on May 21. Along with the some 65 crewmen in

The fire soon spread along the upper decks to the anti-aircraft guns, the ammunition of which shortly started to explode. However, with more time available than on the *Kybfels*, it was possible to effect an orderly evacuation of crew and passengers. This picture of the burning and sinking *Marburg* drifting south towards the shores of Ithaki was taken from one the lifeboats. (Archivio Centrale dello Stato)

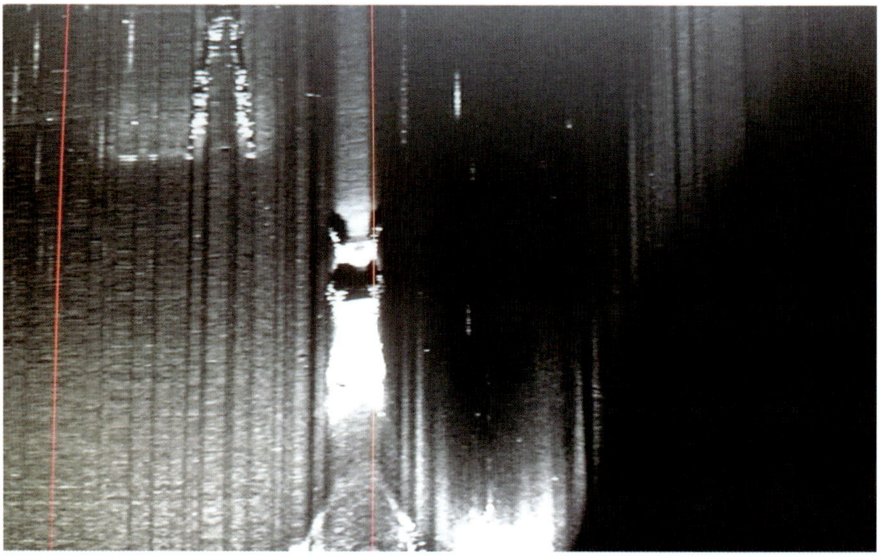

The last resting place of the *Marburg* was discovered by Greek seabed researcher Gerasimos Sotiropoulos in 2016, sonar images revealing that it lay at a depth of 300 metres and had broken into two pieces. (Gerasimos Sotiropoulos)

each ship, this added up 1,408. Out of these, a total of 1,155 survived, with 56 confirmed dead, leaving another 197 unaccounted for. Total losses by the division were later reported as two officers, five NCOs and 33 men drowned, while three officers, 33 NCOs and 108 men were reported missing – a total loss of 184 men.

More serious was the loss of vehicles, guns and other equipment (180 on the *Kybfels* and 175 on the *Marburg*) – including ten heavy armoured reconnaissance cars, five light, 50 medium and five heavy half-tracks, 16 field howitzers, ten 10.5cm and four 15cm guns and 14 self-propelled 3.7cm and four self-propelled 2cm quadruple Flak guns – which could only be replaced once the division returned to Germany.

The original intention had been for the 2. Panzer-Division to take part in Operation 'Barbarossa', the invasion of the Soviet Union in June. Instead it remained as an OKH reserve in the Lemberg–Przemysl area until August 10, when it was transferred to the La Rochelle–Bordeaux region in France to act as an occupation force there. Thus it was not until September that it began its move over to the Smolensk area on the Eastern Front.

ANATOMY OF A PYRRHIC VICTORY

IN RETROSPECT IT COULD be said that neither the British Commonwealth nor the German forces performed particularly well during the fighting at the Pineios gorge. In the case of the Anzacs much criticism has focused on the 21st NZ Battalion and its commander, Lieutenant-Colonel Macky, over their part in that battle. This is because after successfully holding Platamon ridge for 36 hours, 12 hours longer than Freyberg thought possible, albeit sans 2-pounder anti-tank guns, and pulling out with minimal casualties, Macky's defence of the Pineios gorge appeared to fall apart very quickly. This view appears to have started around the time of the preparation of the New Zealand official history of the campaign, much of the criticism coming from the Editor-in-Chief of the official war history series, Howard Kippenberger (who himself had commanded the 20th NZ Battalion in the 4th NZ Brigade during the campaign), and seems to have been picked up by all authors since. But is it fair?

Macky's primary mistake has been put down to his failure to adequately prepare for and deal with an attack by tanks from the gorge. This is curious because it would appear that Anzac Corps Headquarters was not prepared for such an eventuality either. In fact Lieutenant-General Blamey and the rest of his headquarters considered the Platamon/Pineios position to be impregnable, though it is not clear why. At least one New Zealand officer noted that a map in his possession indicated that the river was too deep for tanks to cross, making it essentially a natural anti-tank trap. Concurrently with this, most post-war accounts and maps refer to the existence of a ford in the middle of the gorge, thought this appears to be based on a German combat report. In fact no part of the river at that point in the gorge fits the definition of a ford. One of the only places suitable for a crossing was the river terrace around the church of Agia Paraskevi, the drop off from the railway embankment either side of this terrace being unsuitable for tanks as the slope down was too steep and terminated in the river itself. Certainly, the German tanks forded the river but travelling 200 metres upstream hardly fits the description of a ford and was certainly something that no one could have possibly foreseen.

The early withdrawal of the battalion's No. 10 Platoon from the gorge has been another focus of concern, particularly as their orders were to prevent the Germans from repairing the road. How they were supposed to do this

Of the total of 62,500 British, Australian and New Zealand troops that had been deployed to the Greek mainland, nearly 14,000 were taken prisoner by the Germans. At Kalamata alone, nearly 8,000 were left behind after the conclusion of the evacuation on May 1. Here a large group of them await their fate on the quayside.

when faced by tanks with frontal armour impervious to anti-tank rifle is not clear. It is possible that the platoon could have provided advanced warning that the Germans were sending tanks over the river but, while they heard them cross the river, neither they nor the Australian patrol in the gorge were in a position to actually see the tanks crossing, instead reporting that infantry had crossed instead.

The rapid collapse of the 21st NZ Battalion once the tanks broke out of the gorge has been a second source of contention. The Australians were particularly upset to see the New Zealanders starting to ascend the slopes above Tempi and were left with the impression that the battalion had just given up. Questions have been asked as to how a small force of tanks and infantry could have so easily overcome an entire battalion but in reality there was little they could really do against the tanks, other than the action taken. Chilton's 2/2nd Australian Battalion responded in the same fashion when confronted by tanks. With no field telephone lines Macky's only way of communicating with his troops was by way of runners, something risky at the best of times but made more difficult on the steep, sparsely vegetated slopes below Ambelakia. Macky's use of Very lights to signal his companies to withdraw was a novel way of dealing with a difficult situation. When considering the overall defence of the gorge by the 21st Battalion,

Those captured at Kalamata were initially held in barrack camps in the town. (USNA StP 151-07)

From there, over the next several days, they were transferred by train to a large camp at Corinth where about 10,000 prisoners were assembled, including 350 officers. Here a group makes ready to leave Kalamata. (USNA StP 151-17)

one thing is apparent. They managed to slow the advance of Aufklärungs-Abteilung 112, the unit taking ten hours to secure Tempi, while it took just over three hours for the panzers to reach them there. This was hardly a rapid collapse of a unit. Balck took another hour to assemble a breakout force of tanks from Tempi and then it took another half hour to overcome the last company of the battalion. Ultimately it was these delays that cost Kampfgruppe Balck their chance of reaching Larissa by nightfall.

Looking further up the chain of command, Blamey's overall behaviour at this critical time needs to be called into question. The decision to send a battalion from the 16th Australian Brigade to Tempi, and not Zarkos as originally intended, came very late and was made not by him but by his Chief-of-Staff, Brigadier Rowell. This also came after Rowell had first ordered Brigadier Clowes to investigate the situation. Just why it was felt necessary to do this and not to trust the radio messages they had been receiving is perhaps the strangest part of the whole episode. Apparently there was a general feeling at Anzac Corps Headquarters that Macky was 'in a blue funk'. Time at this point was of the essence and sending a brigadier on a personal mission also made little sense, especially when no one at Anzac Corps HQ knew the best way to get to Platamon! Nor could Clowes provide Macky with any reassurance that reinforcements were on

The men were lining op on Navarinou Street, the sea boulevard at the eastern end of the built-up area. (Google)

their way. His order to Macky to hold the gorge 'to extinction' if necessary was hardly one to inspire confidence.

The delay in the dispatch of reinforcements to the Platamon/Pineios position needs to be questioned as well. Under similar circumstances the Germans would have responded immediately, scraping together what units they had nearby and dispatching them to the threatened area as soon as they could. There were clearly enough uncommitted artillery and anti-tank units in the area. The only reliable cruiser tanks were close by with Savige Force at Kalabaka and six of them were still mobile. At least one battalion could be drawn from the 6th NZ Brigade further south at Elasson, while the 2/7th Australian Battalion was on its way up by train from Domokos, albeit under the control of General Wilson who knew nothing of this deteriorating situation thanks to Blamey. The re-assignment of the battalions to the defence of the gorge was also sloppy to say the least and became chaotic at a critical time in preparing for this defence. It is not even clear why Blamey deemed it necessary to establish three blocking groups on his western flank when there was no tangible threat from that direction, while a single battalion was facing a major incursion from a panzer division in the east.

Just why Wilson was excluded from the flow of information is curious. Blamey might have resented Wilson taking control of two Australian

A mixture of British, New Zealanders and Greeks being marched off to the railway station under guard. (NIOD 21074)

battalions but it could be deeper than that. It is possible that Blamey, harbouring resentment over the appointment of Wilson to overall command of Operation 'Lustre', a role he felt entitled to, may have led him to feel that he had finally got the command he had been denied. There is certainly the feeling that Blamey appears to be the sort of man who was not averse to letting personal grievances get in the way of good decision-making. There is a view among Australian officers that his personal enmity towards Lieutenant-General Lavarack was behind his insistence that the 6th Australian Division, and not Lavarack's 7th, was sent first to Greece. In the end he escaped censure because the Anzac Corps successfully escaped the trap and others took the blame. Of them, Macky fared the worst. Hospitalised on his return to the division in Greece, most probably for post-traumatic stress disorder, he was forced to relinquish command of the 21st Battalion on Crete and finally sacked by Freyberg/Hargest on the division's return to Egypt. Chilton did not escape unscathed either. He was admonished for his untimely abandonment of Evangelismos and withdrawal over Mount Ossa.

Of all the engagements of the Greek campaign, the twin battles of Platamon ridge and the Pineios gorge would have to have been the most critical. This was because around the time the first troops from Kampfgruppe Balck reached Platamon on April 14 the entire New Zealand Division and half of the 6th Australian Division were arrayed along the Olympus-Aliákmon Line, their only route of escape being through the town of Larissa. This was also the preferred escape route of Savige Force and the British 1st Armoured Brigade because of the poor condition of the more-direct route from Trikkala to Domokos. Thus, by the time of close of battle on April 16, with the tunnel effectively closed for days, the only thing that stood in the way of Kampfgruppe Balck and Larissa was the saddle track, the latter lined with anti-tank mines acquired by dubious means from the British Army in the UK. This was one occasion when the New Zealand soldier's propensity for looting paid off.

Fortunately the Australian and New Zealand governments never did find out how close they had come to losing their valued contributions to the war, The British government itself did not find out either, apparently because Wilson did not learn of the fighting at the Pineios gorge until he had all but completed his own report after he got back to Egypt. Instead all the New Zealand government was told was that three major battles had been fought in Greece, specifically on Olympus Pass, at Thermopylae and near Grevena! Curiously no fighting ever took place around the latter.

During the battle of Asculum in 279 BC Pyrrhus of Epirus defeated the Roman forces but in the process destroyed most of his own army, forcing the end of his campaign. Based on his own quote a Pyrrhic victory has been defined as: 'A victory that inflicts such a devastating toll on the victor that it is tantamount to a defeat. Such a victory negates any true sense of achievement or damages long-term progress.' Could the battle of the Pineios gorge be defined as such?

In the case of the 2. Panzer-Division, it could be said that whatever their experiences were in Poland and then France, these could not have prepared them for what they were to encounter in Greece or against the Anzacs. This could be put down to a number of factors, which dogged them throughout their entire operations in Greece, among them a lack of appreciation of the terrain and the quality of the country's road network.

The first inkling the 2. Panzer-Division had of this was on their drive from Strumica in Yugoslavia through to Salonika, the muddy roads causing considerable delays. After reaching Salonika on April 9, Balck was optimistically expecting to receive replenishments in another 48 hours but it would be another two days before his tanks became mobile again. Things were not better further south. What New Zealand troops encountered in the valley of the Aliákmon river were what they described as 'little more than deep-rutted cart tracks, which were likely to turn impassable in the rain thanks to the clay of which they were composed'. Nor did these roads stand up to heavy traffic, time and time again compromising the 2. Panzer-Division's efforts to resupply its forward units. The numerous demolitions left behind by the New Zealanders as they retreated further complicated this. Time and time again it was this combination of poor

Prisoners boarding the train that will take them north to Corinth as the first leg on their way to four unhappy years as prisoners of war in Germany. (NIOD 21089)

roads and demolitions that held up the advance of Kampfgruppe Balck and compromised their ability to cut off sizable numbers of enemy troops. Sometimes it was only the capture of an abandoned British supply dump that kept them going with food.

It is also possible that the easy victories in France had made the Germans over-confident. There were occasions in June 1940 when the mere fear of

tanks approaching could send French troops into a panicked retreat. Contrast this with the refusal of No. 13 Platoon of the 21st NZ Battalion to surrender to the three tanks that drove up to their position at the Pineios gorge. A report from the 2. Panzer-Division after the fighting in Greece noted: 'Australian and New Zealand soldiers fought an outstanding defensive battle in the craggy wooded country in which they had to fight. Their choice of ground, use of ground, adaptation of the ground and construction of positions were good and made things very hard for the attackers.' The Germans made up for this by their willingness to operate on the flanks, exploiting avenues of attack that were less expected by W Force. This included using roads considered not suitable for wheeled vehicles let alone tanks, or finding a way across a river considered to be unfordable.

Nevertheless, Balck made two tactical errors during the Pineios gorge fighting. The first of these was to send the entire column into the gorge without first determining if this route was clear. Had he discovered the tunnel demolitions before committing his armour he might have been able to find a way to ford the river at the eastern exit of the gorge. If it had been possible to cross the river there the entire force of tanks could have been ready to break out from the gorge once the craters in the road had been filled in. Having committed the entire force to the railway route their only option was to find a way across the river at the head of the column, as pulling the tanks out of the gorge would have been costly in term of petrol and compromised their efforts to actually reach Larissa.

The second tactical error occurred during the fighting on April 18 when Oberstleutnant Decker committed one of the cardinal sins of modern armoured warfare. In his haste to link up with the mountain troops beyond at Tempi he sent forward what tanks he had over the river, essentially splitting the 1. Kompanie of his I. Abteilung into penny packets. The result was that the tanks were easily destroyed by the New Zealand anti-tank guns, only one reaching Tempi unscathed. Nevertheless, the fording of the river in the centre of the gorge proved to be slow, Balck later claiming: 'Every half hour a tank made it through the river.' In the end it took him till 4.30 p.m. to launch his main thrust out of Tempi and it proved too late for the battlegroup to reach Larissa that night.

In the end though the whole Platamon–Pineios attack proved costly for Kampfgruppe Balck. Theoretically the I. Abteilung of Panzer-Regiment 3 would have started the battle with 54 tanks (20 PzKpfw IIs, 24 PzKpfw IIIs and ten PzKpfw IVs, augmented by five PzKpfw IIs from Regimental Headquarters). By the end of the day their losses had left them with no more than 23 operational tanks. To make matters worse, by the time they reached Larissa all of their medium tanks were out of petrol. Though they did discover the British fuel dump in the town later that day they claimed it was too late for them to pursue the enemy. It would appear that the petrol there was insufficient to maintain the further advance of even a panzer company. Another complicating factor concerns the 9. Panzer-Division, which despite orders not to advance beyond the road fork at Elefterochori, did so, cutting off Panzer-Aufklärungs-Abteilung 5 and possibly also logistical support for the 2. Panzer-Division. Balck's panzers were also short of supporting infantry, the bulk of Schützen-Regiment 304 not arriving till the following day. Nor could he count on Generalmajor Schörner's mountain troops, exhausted after their crossing of the slopes of the Olympus and subsequent fighting. Thus, in a sense, though they had broken through at the Pineios gorge and captured Larissa their inability to pursue the vanquished Anzacs puts this battle in the category of a Pyrrhic victory.

SOURCES

ARCHIVES

Archives New Zealand

WAII 1 119 DA 30/10/1: 2nd New Zealand Expeditionary Force – Headquarters NZ Division (G Branch) – Operations of 'A' Troop, 2nd NZ Division Engineers – 5th NZ Field Regiment in the Platamon Tunnel Engagement in Greece – L.G. Williams.

WAII 1 334 DA 438.21/9–11: German Army Documents on the Greek Campaign.

WAII 1 334 DA 438.21 9–11: 6. Gebirgs-Division Kriegstagebuch (War Diary), April 1941.

WAII 1 349 DA 447.21/1–44: Eyewitness accounts. The Action at Pineios Gorge, Greece. Extract from book written by Sergeant Uren, 4th NZ Field Regiment.

WAII 1 1655 DA 54/1/15-18: 21st NZ Battalion War Diary, March-June 1941.

WAII 3/1/7: Campaign in Greece,1941. Correspondence files 21st NZ Battalion.

WAII 3/1/7: Greece 1941, correspondence files 21st NZ Battalion 1945-1960, Lieutenant M.C. O'Neill, No. 13 Platoon, C Company, 21st Battalion.

WAII DA 30/10/11: 5th NZ Field Regiment Summary of Operations in Greece, April 1941.

WAII DA 32/10/14: No. 1 Troop, 3rd Battery, 7th Anti-Tank Regiment, Pineios Gorge.

181/32/6: War History – Authors – W.G. McClymont.

Australian War Memorial

AWM52 1/5/162: 6th Australian Division General Staff Branch, March-April 1941.

AWM52 8/2/16/7: 16th Infantry Brigade, March-April 1941.

AWM52 8/3/1/13: 2/1st Infantry Battalion, March-May 1941.

AWM52 8/3/2/19: 2/2nd Infantry Battalion, April 1941.

AWM52 8/3/3/8: 2/3rd Infantry Battalion, December 1940-June 1941.

AWM52 8/5/3/6: 2/5th Infantry Battalion, April-June 1941.

AWM52 8/3/6/9: 2/6th Infantry Battalion, February-June 1941.

AWM52 8/3/7: 2/7th Infantry Battalion, April-June 1941.

AWM52 8/3/11/10: 2/11th Infantry Battalion, April-June 1941.

AWM52 8/4/1: I Australian Corps General Branch, March-May 1941.

AWM52 4/1/5/3: 2/1st HQ RAA I Australian Corps, January-May 1941.

AWM52 4/4/1/4: 2/1st Anti-Tank Regiment, April-June 1941.

AWM52 4/2/2/16: 2/2nd Field Regiment, March-July 1941.

AWM52 5/13/1/10: 2/1st Field Company RAE, April 1941.

NX2274: Corporal Jack Codrington, My Life as a Soldier.

3DRL 6763A: Sydney Rowell Papers, The Campaign in Greece, April 1941.

The National Archives (UK)

DEFE 3/891: Intelligence from intercepted German, Italian and Japanese radio communications, WWII, March-April 23, 1941.

WO 69/994B: General Headquarters (GHQ): HQ British Troops Greece, March-April 1941.

WO 201/53: Greece: Commander-in-Chief's Report on Operations April 1941.

WO 169/1268: HQ 1st Armoured Brigade War Diary, January-November 1941.

WO 169/1141: 3rd Royal Tank Regiment War Diary, January-April 1941.

National Archives and Records Administration (US)

2. Panzer-Division Kriegstagebuch (War Diary), April-May 1941.

I./Panzer-Regiment 3. Gefechtsbericht über die Zeit vom 15.-19.4.1941.

Gefechtsbericht des Panzer-Regiments 3 für die Zeit vom 15.-19.4.1941.

BOOKS

Balck, Hermann: *Order in Chaos. The Memoirs of General of Panzer Troops Hermann Balck* (University Press of Kentucky, Lexington, 2015).

Beevor, Anthony: *Crete. The Battle and the Resistance* (Penguin, London, 1991).

Bennett, Ralph: *Ultra and Mediterranean Strategy* (William Morrow, New York, 1989).

Borman, Clifford Allan: *Divisional Signals. Official History of New Zealand in the Second World War 1939-45* (War History Branch, Department of Internal Affairs, New Zealand, 1954).

Cody, Joseph Frederick: *21 Battalion. Official History of New Zealand in the Second World War 1939-45* (War History Branch, Department of Internal Affairs, New Zealand, 1953).

Cody, Joseph Frederick: *New Zealand Engineers, Middle East. Official History of New Zealand in the Second World War 1939-45.* (War History Branch, Department of Internal Affairs, New Zealand, 1961).

Crisp, Robert: *The Gods Were Neutral: A British Tank Officer's Very Personal Account of the Ill-Fated Greek Campaign in WWII* (Frederick Muller, London, 1960).

Deed, Philip: *2nd New Zealand Divisional Cavalry. Men with No. 1 Troop and B Squadron 1939-1942, Mediterranean* (Inhouse Design and Print, Matamata, 2018).

Documents Relating to New Zealand's Participation in the Second World War 1939-45, Volume I (Government Printer, Wellington, New Zealand, 1949).

Ewer, Peter: Forgotten Anzacs. *The Campaign in Greece 1941* (Scribe Publications, Carlton, NSW, Australia, 2008).

Givney, Edwyn Charles: *The First at War. The Story of the 2/1st Infantry Battalion 1939-45, the City of Sydney Regiment* (Association of First Infantry Battalions, Editorial Committee, 1987).

Golla, Karl-Heinz: *Der Fall Griechenland 1941* (Mittler-Verlag, Hamburg, 2007)

Hinsley, F. Harry: *British Intelligence in the Second World War, Volume 1* (Her Majesty's Stationery Office, London, 1979).

Horner, David: *High Command. Australia and Allied Strategy 1939-1945* (Allen & Unwin, Sydney, 1982).

Horner, David: *Blamey: The Commander-in-Chief* (Allen & Unwin, Sydney, 1998).

Long, Gavin: *Greece, Crete and Syria. Australia in the War of 1939-1945. Series 1 – Army, Volume II* (Australian War Memorial, Canberra, 1953).

Loughnan, Robert J. M.: *Divisional Cavalry. Official History of New Zealand in the Second World War 1939-45* (War History Branch, Department of Internal Affairs, New Zealand, 1963).

McClymont, William Graham: *To Greece. Official History of New Zealand in the Second World War 1939-45* (War History Branch, Department of Internal Affairs, New Zealand, 1959).

Murphy, Walter Edward: *2nd New Zealand Divisional Artillery. Official History of New Zealand in the Second World War 1939-45* (War History Branch, Department of Internal Affairs, New Zealand, 1966).

Playfair, Major-General I. S. O.: *The Mediterranean and the Middle East, Volume I: The Early Successes Against Italy (to May 1941)* (Her Majesty's Stationery Office, London, 1954).

Playfair, Major-General I. S. O.: *The Mediterranean and the Middle East, Volume II: The Germans come to the Help of their Ally (1941)* (Her Majesty's Stationery Office, London, 1956).

Plato, Anton Detlev von: *Die Geschichte der 5. Panzerdivision 1938-1945* (Walhalla und Praetoria Verlag, Regensburg, 1978).

Reid, R. J. M.: *Recollections of Greece March-April 1941. 1939-1946: 2/3 Infantry Battalion A.I.F.* (Beverly Hills, NSW, F. Reid, 1999).

Rowell, Sir Sydney: *Full Circle.* (Melbourne University Press, Carlton, 1974).

Ruef, Karl: *Gebirgsjäger zwischen Kreta und Murmansk. Die Schicksale der 6. Gebirgsdivision* (Leopold Stocker Verlag, Graz, 1970).

Steinzer Franz: *Die 2. Panzer-Division 1939-1945: Bewaffnung, Einsätze, Männer* (Podzun-Pallas-Verlag, Friedberg, 1982).

Trigellis-Smith, Syd: *All the King's Enemies. A History of the 2/5th Australian Infantry Battalion* (2/5th Battalion Association, 1988).

Wick, Stan: *Purple over Green. The History of 2/2nd Australian Infantry Battalion 1939-1945* (2/2nd Australian Infantry Battalion Association, 1977).

ARTICLES

Kitzmüller: 'Schlacht am Olymp, Der Kampf der 2. Pz. Div mit dem britischen Expeditionskorps April 1941', in *Mitteilungsblatt der Kameradschaft der 2. Panzer-Division* (1964), pp 6-8.

Vogias, Charalambos: *The truth about the destruction of the old stone bridge of Larissa by New Zealanders in 1941 and Germans in 1944* (Academia, 2016).

PERSONAL ACCOUNTS

Lieutenant Harry Capamagain, Diary.

Sapper Francis Clive Lowe, Diary.